Stewards
of
Excellence

Stewards
of
Excellence

Leadership Strategies
for a Successful Military Transition to a
Rewarding Civilian Career

Roderick D. Steward

M. Patrice Group LLC
Wesley Chapel, NC 28173
704-256-3789

First Edition
Design and production management by MPG
Editor: Melanie Calloway

Library of Congress Control Number: 2017906036
ISBN: 978-0-9965190-4-5   Hardcover
        978-0-9965190-5-2   Paperback
        978-0-9965190-6-9   eBook

CONTENTS

CONTENTS

DEDICATION

I dedicate this book to the past, present, and future guardians of our nation. Were it not for the courage, commitment, and sacrifice of these brave men and women, the United States of America would not be.

ACKNOWLEDGEMENTS

Nineteenth-century novelist Owen Wister wrote, "It was neither preaching nor praying that made a better man of me, but one or two people who believed in me better than I deserved, and I hated to disappoint them."

I might have occasionally disappointed them, but I owe a debt of eternal gratitude for living a legacy of valor bequeathed to me by both my mother and grandmother. Each provided a watchful eye over me and were first to encourage me to enlist in the military. Without their undying love and support, many of my accomplishments would be for nothing. Thank you, Elaine Earl and Eleanor Cockrell.

I also extend a lifelong thank you to other ladies who helped guide my extraordinary life's journey: N'Shana, Anitra, and Sabrun. You are the sugar honey iced tea! For so long, I have depended on you as my foundation. I could not have made it through my life in the military without your unconditional love and support. Thank you for accompanying me on this incredible journey. There is so much more to come!

Surely, I would be remiss if I did not acknowledge the person who helped bring this book to life. What you now hold in your hands is the result of months of corrections, additions, deletions, research, and yes, more revisions. A monumental task was made easier with Melanie's talent for turning my fragmented thoughts and early drafts into a complete manuscript.

Lastly, after multiple tours of duty and reenlistments in the United States Air Force, I retired with twenty-one years of honorable service to my country. My retirement was not without ceremony; associates honored me for my service with a celebration fit for a leader. I had, in every estimation, attained the admiration of my peers and subordinates alike. Without pomp nor circumstance, I lived up to the Airmen's Creed which states, "I am an American Airman. Wingman, Leader, Warrior." So, with admiration to the many friends, supervisors, formal and informal leaders who have molded me into the self-assured, confident leader I have become, I extend a sincere note of thanks.

INTRODUCTION

I have been living the pages of this book for the past twenty-five years when, as a naïve 18-year-old I joined the military. While enlisted, I learned a lot about myself and those around me. One of the important lessons I reaped from my extraordinary experiences in the Armed Forces is that I should dismiss as a way of thinking the need to please everyone. The focus should be on the reason we are all here—for something greater than ourselves.

The book you hold in your hands was developed from a creed I have adhered to throughout my time in the military: service before self. I wrote with two audiences in mind. First, the transitioning military professional and second, civilians who want to learn more about the many benefits former military members can offer to private organizations. I only wish a book like this was available to me before I retired from active duty; my transition would have been smoother than I experienced.

Over the years, a lot has been written about leadership by authorities such as John Maxwell, Seth Godin, Jim Rohn, Steven Covey, Jack Welch, and others. These same contemporary experts rely on the experiences of earlier pioneers like Napoleon Hill and Dale Carnegie. Inc Magazine contributing editor Jeff Haden wrote an article[i] naming the top 101 leadership and management experts. His list scratches the surface of an ever-increasing roster of men and women who know one must exhibit leadership qualities front and center to experience success. Many of the individuals have achieved international acclaim, while others have gained renown on a national or local scale. The one shared quality they possess, as Jeff Haden notes, "is they use the ideas, the perspectives, and the advice of others as the basis for their thoughts and actions.

My practices are disciplined, hard-earned, and time-honored. Thus, I have compiled an outline for you to use in your military transition based on the lessons, guidance, and experiences I have gleaned during my time spent in the United States Air Force. If you adhere to the prescribed plan of action, I believe you will have an easier time making the transition from military to the public or private sector and possibly land a better-paying, rewarding civilian job. This method worked well for me, and I know it will work for you.

If you are like the thousands of men and women who have been out of the job market for several years, you will want to "use the ideas and perspectives of others" to fine tune and personalize your job seeking practices. Resources abound to help you in your quest for meaningful employment after the military. While I have provided you with a way and means, you must do the legwork.

As you move through each stage summarized in the book, measure your progress. Just remember that snagging an interview is not the only barometer of a success. A job offer for your preferred position at your desired salary will be the ultimate reward for persistence and your ability to stay single-minded and focused on the task at hand—*preparation*. Abraham Lincoln wisely stated, "Give me six hours to chop down a tree, and I will spend the first four sharpening the ax."

Keep in mind, a successful transition begins months, even years before you leave the military. You must grind your ax by gathering quality information, and then, by evaluating your probability of success utilizing the strategies shared in each chapter.

Chapter One is for both enlisted and officer corps, and those in the private sector who want to understand how military culture influences the civilian world and how that culture directly impacts relationships between the average military and civilian managers. Discussed also are the various facets of leadership and how different styles influenced my training and career path.

Chapter Two is for present and former military members who are transitioning to the civilian sector. Understanding separation myths, how to prepare yourself for your new assignment as a civilian, and how to maintain focus when things go not as planned are topics you will want to refer often. This comprehensive chapter teaches the "Steward Methodology": how to devise and execute your transition and regularly evaluating your progress, making corrections or changes where necessary. Refer to this chapter often because it offers a precise blueprint for success.

Individuals interviewed for this book have many commonalities, most apparent the need for the military professional to trust but verify information. Chapter Three uses case studies to show us how to make the VA claim process easier. If you, like me and the other men and women featured in the following chapters, have had challenging or questionable interactions with the Office of Veteran Affairs, this section offers a fool-proof way to navigate through the bureaucracy.

The overarching theme throughout the book is pre-paring for a leadership role in the civilian workforce, not just landing a J-O-B. Chapter Four examines the unique demands and unmatched benefits of military leader-ship. We explore core values and the role those ethics play in everyday interactions among recently separated military and their civilian counterparts. How might corporations benefit by employing men and women with military-acquired leadership traits? We explore this question.

Chapter Five helps military and civilian employees understand the win-lose dichotomy found in both mili-tary and civilian settings. In behavioral economics, there is a concept know as loss aversion[ii] which refers directly to a person's tendency to prefer avoiding losses rather than acquiring similar gains. It considers the importance of performance measurement—that is—setting and evaluating goals. When we set goals, the focus is often on the benefits we will attain from achieving them.

Goals are like a game of darts—measurable. When you strike a grid on the dartboard, you score points. If you hit a bullseye, you are ahead of the game. When you miss the mark, points get deducted. The more times you miss the mark, the more points you must relinquish.

Similarly, loss aversion teaches us we also need to take into consideration the career and life points we will *lose* if we do not reach our goals.

Chapter Six explores the intrinsic value of military members. Most military professionals do not know the worth of their unique skill set in the civilian job market. Salary and salary negotiation is a subject left unexplored before and after we separate from the military. These rarely taught, yet important topics are lacking in the Transition Assistance Program (TAP) sessions. I did not have a clue I could negotiate my salary! We will delve into myriad ways to determine your employment worth.

Each chapter ends with a takeaway, leaving room for questions and exploration. Reflect on the summary and write down steps that will propel you closer to your objective.

I have also put together a resource library of suggested readings, military-friendly companies, websites, and more that will be useful in your new life.

Your ascent into the civilian world is just beginning. Adhering to the steps found in each chapter will assist you in your decision to lead with purpose and excellence. I have every confidence you will discover traits you did not know you possessed. In so doing, you will uncover the secret to having a successful military transition and a rewarding civilian career.

Roderick D. Steward
April 2017

CHAPTER ONE

THE LEADERSHIP CONUNDRUM

"A true
leader has the
confidence to stand alone,
the courage to make tough decisions,
and the compassion to listen to the needs of
others. He does not set out to be
a leader, but becomes one by
the equality of his actions
and the integrity of
his intent."
Douglas MacArthur

Early in my career, I was told military officers are trained to believe the enlisted must be led to be effective. However, throughout my 21 years as an active duty Airman, I have witnessed numerous enlisted professionals adeptly "leading" their way up the ladder to gain rank.

Many of those individuals did not have what some consider the benefit or "privilege" of attending military preparatory schools. These professionals achieved position and grade with experience, aptitude, determination to excel, and more importantly, an intense desire to be of service. The willingness to serve is a defining aspect of military life as well as the number one prerequisite most civilian institutions require when prospecting for qualified candidates.

In JFK's oft-quoted inaugural address he compels us to "ask not what your country can do for you, ask what you can do for your country." Former enlisted professionals answer this call willingly. Not only do we, the enlisted, lead effectively, but we also have a deeper understanding of what it is like to execute the tasks a subordinate is likely to perform.

Responsibility levels for the enlisted is directly related to the length of time he or she has spent in the military. A first tier (O-1) officer immediately gets put in charge of personnel and property. A first tier enlisted (E-1) earns his or her supervisory status through years of active duty before he or she elevates to first tier manager (one who received training or has experience managing or leading people). This "on-the-job training" equips the enlisted to guide those under his or her charge with a transformative, yet empathetic hand.

The military has transformation down to a science. For hundreds of years, it has groomed our citizen civilians into citizen warriors through training, education, and discipline. The various schools range from six weeks to several months and cram in a lot of instruction. The Marine Corps' Recruit Training program is thirteen weeks long; the Army's basic training program is ten weeks; the Navy's boot camp is eight, and the Air Force's basic military training (BMT) is seven weeks long.

Newly minted service members then attend training in their primary military occupational specialty (MOS) or Air Force Specialty Code (AFSC). My military education was life changing; I am wiser and better for having gone through it! The immersive level of instruction and clear expectations adequately prepared me for my official military duties.

Part of the training curriculum the United States Air Force has is the Leaders Encouraging Airman Development program (LEAD) which is designed to offer the best and brightest enlisted professionals the opportunity to become commissioned officers. The moment you start BMT, you are taught about the upper echelon of the Air Force. Instructors teach you to believe you could one day be a member of that hallowed space. Given to each are real-world challenges and hands-on drills that push us beyond our limits and equip us for the rigors of leadership.

One may also choose to take an academic route. Available to select recruits is the US Air Force Academy and comparable educational institutes. These persons are disciplined from the onset to become officers of character. Academyadmissions.com asserts, "Prior-enlisted cadets attending the Academy and its Preparatory School are indisputably amongst the best the Air Force has to offer."[iii] Cadets are pushed physically, mentally, and emotionally to their limited capacities. Certainly, these are traits demanded of any serviceman.

Does this mean only academy graduates and those attending elite training programs succeed as leaders? Let's explore that thought.

The enlisted experience gives the modern-day professional understanding and respect of the sacrifices required to master a task. It also offers a wealth of leadership strengths that tie everything together as one prepares for his or her civilian transition. Those rich experiences are at the heart of what separates the enlisted from the civilian.

Think about it; for whom would you rather work: a person who has only overseen paper rather than people, or someone who has enthusiastically led the charge with a "been-to-hell-and-back-type attitude?" For me, that is an easy decision, in part because I have seen the marginalization of the hands-on experience gap and promotional disparity between the NCO and Officer corps.

As an example, for an officer to get promoted, he or she must adhere to Title 10, United States Code (USC). There are many factors prescribed under this law, but the road to promotion for an officer is distinctively different than for that of an enlisted member of the armed services.

Commanders recommend commissioned officers for promotion. Next, they go for review before promotions boards who make upgrade determinations based largely on the officers' fitness reports, and his or her level of responsibility in their respective assignments.

In contrast, for an enlisted to get promoted, one must score high on a specialty knowledge examination and pass a fitness assessment (PT test). He must meet minimum time requirements in his current rank, have a certain number of years of total military service, *and* have high marks on his Enlisted Performance Report (EPR). This report is like an annual review in the civilian world.

Certain branches of the military require the enlisted to go before a promotions board where, unlike the officers' board, one must answer a litany of pre-established questions to determine promotability.

Ultimately, members of both groups, former officers and the enlisted, when given the opportunity, are exceptional additions to high-performance teams. Regardless of status, each have invaluable leadership and management capabilities. The private enterprise is wise not to overlook the beneficial characteristics each group possesses.

Differences between officer and enlisted was once explained to me using parts of the human anatomy. Described as the backbone of the military is the noncommissioned officer corps. With that accepted as true, an officer could then be considered the brain, and the junior enlisted professional, the body.

The officers using "their brains" set the vision and mission, and the NCOs take the vision and translate it into specific tasks which their teams execute, making the mission a reality. The NCOs lead and manage the junior enlisted who do the work. Without the brain (officers) the body cannot function. Without the backbone (NCOs) the body also cannot function. But, without a body, there is no need for a brain nor a spine. All must work together harmoniously for the success of the operation.

Why does this separation exist? As a rule, in the military, we see officers take *command* of their subordinates while the enlisted take *charge* of their subordinates. Both have their merits. Taking command relies on confident, decisive, sometimes bold leadership prowess that says, "follow me." Taking charge, on the other hand, is based on metered control. Persian Gulf War General Norman Schwarzkopf best defined the correlation between the two when he said, "When placed in command, take charge." Officer or enlisted, whether brain, backbone, or body, each contributes to the safety and well-being of our nation.

Many rightly believe we need abolishment of the age-old system separating the volunteer officer and enlisted corps. The Greek historian Thucydides wrote, "The Nation that makes a great distinction between its scholars and its warriors will have its thinking done by cowards and its fighting done by fools." For this very reason, today's military system should not separate of-

ficer and enlisted before each proves him or herself worthy of a title. A combination of education, training, *and*
experience should be the determinant for who is best
suited to hold leadership positions.

These vague distinctions in "stature" at times per-
meate from officers to their families with a misguided
sense of privilege. I was amazed at the treatment select
military husbands and wives received. It was if they had
attained the rank of their spouses. Not for nothing but—
WTF?

To my dismay, this sense of privilege also exists in
the local communities around military installations.
Like it or not, people who own and rent homes to military families in many cases cater to officers over enlisted
professionals, even if the enlisted in need held a senior
position and was in service to his country twice as long.

Why do I mention the treatment disparity between
the enlisted corps and officers and their families? I bring
this up to draw attention to the pervasive effect military
culture has on the private workforce.

Typically, when the civilian organization hears that
Candidate-A was an officer who graduated from military academy A or Reserve Officer Training Corps
(ROTC) program B they automatically believe they have
something special. Now enters Candidate-C, who just
returned from a tour of duty in Iraq, enlisted for the
same length of time as the commissioned Candidate-A.
Who is more likely to get the job? In my vast experience,
I have found Candidate A usually lands the job.

I would like to think the criteria for hiring and promoting a person to a leadership position on a job is

based on the level of experience needed to perform the job best and the integrity of the individual.

From basic military training to retirement, to a Lean Six Sigma Black Belt, to my position as Senior Lean Executive Coach I have been afforded the practical knowledge to offer insights into the operations of not only organizational leaders but rank-and-file also.

> Reading books can increase a persons' intelligence but years of work experience can take brainpower and make it actionable.

Simply put, there are things one cannot learn in school through book, lecture, or conjecture; only experience can offer such beneficial insights. Let it be known, there is no substitute for a military members tried-and-true experiences and courage under fire.

The powerful life lessons that make former military men and women qualified for their service to others should be the prerequisite for employment at any level. Those rich, authentic experiences weave the fabric of our nation and are what adds texture to any organization. It is what inspires me to help others realize their leadership potential in the private sector. That is what keeps *me* up at night.

The thoughts presented in this book are not only my experiences but those of other servicemen and women who have experienced intense, teachable moments as they bravely put their lives in harm's way in service to our nation. These individuals have labored within the ranks of the military as well as the civilian workforce. Their experiences, while unique, crisscross age, culture, gender, and race. I share Michelle's story to illustrate this point. You, like I, may see a little of yourself or someone you know in her poignant narrative.

After completing two years of undergraduate study at Temple University, Michelle joined the United States Air Force. Her decision to enlist was due in part to her inability to afford tuition costs on her own and her parent's refusal to pay if she was not getting 3.0 GPA or above.

While in school, Michelle partied when she should have been studying. She got mixed up with a guy who was no good for her, and her grades suffered. Eventually, things started to unravel.

Her work-study assignment placed her as a clerk at Temple University Hospital GYN Oncology Department. The atmosphere in the oncology unit was gloomy. That, on top of personal problems, was enough to push her close to the edge. Michelle soon realized she could not continue in the direction she was headed, so two years in, she left Philadelphia and returned home.

Michelle worked odd jobs for a while, but soon realized she did not want to stay at dead-end careers or stay home any longer than necessary. As she complained to a work associate one day, he suggested she join the army reserve.

She had often wondered what it would be like to serve her country in a way that felt like she was contributing to something bigger than herself; to live differently from what she had known for the past twenty years. After conferring with family members who had served in various military branches, Michelle decided on the Air Force and scheduled an appointment with a recruiter.

During her consultation, the recruiter told her she would travel and see the world, have school paid for, medical expenses covered, and have a regular paycheck. He glamorized life in the Air Force, and it sounded great! While Michelle did not fall for everything he said, the promise of free schooling was enticing. Weighing her options against everything he was presenting, enlisting in the United States Air Force seemed to be the best choice at that uncertain time in her life.

A few days later, she returned to take the Armed Services Vocational Aptitude Battery Test (ASVAB) which is used to determine qualifications for enlistments. Unlike the Scholastic Aptitude Test (SAT) you are tested on various talents and natural inclinations. Her highest scores were in finance, medical, and firefighter or police.

Michelle entered the Air Force "open-general," which meant whenever there was a need that mirrored her desired field, she could sign a contract to enlist. Three weeks later, the Air Force identified a need. Michelle said goodbye to family and friends and left for San Antonio, Texas to begin her military career.

After basic training, she selected her job assignment and off to Wichita Falls, Texas she went. In Technical school, she trained in financial management. Michelle discovered she liked working with numbers and she started getting excited about her future.

Shortly after arriving in Texas, she met her future husband. Michelle and David married right after tech school. She was twenty-one, he twenty-four. They soon realized that the uncertainties of military life can cast unforgiving shadows on the youthful glow of love. It was only months after meeting that Michelle's fiancé left for McChord AFB in Lakewood, WA., separating the two for the first time. Michelle left for Offutt AFB in Omaha, Nebraska. There she became part of a large community of newly minted servicemen and women who marry young and find themselves alone.

Married life had its challenges; but, life in the military had more. When Michelle and her husband relocated from McChord to Ramstein AFB in Germany, her new norm as a married woman in a new country was unsettling. Her husband was of German descent, so he was eager to get to know his roots and family. Meanwhile, Michelle was still getting to know him, life in a foreign country, and a new job.

In the end, the adjustment became perhaps as hard on her marriage as it was on her job. Marital problems had Michelle keeping a lot bottled up, and her non-verbals at work resulted in counsel. The communication was even worse at home. When expressing herself, she was either misunderstood or seen as coming off angry. Michelle soon found out her husband was cheating on her. Who wouldn't be mad? To say they had problems would be an understatement.

Years later Michelle realized she could have received individual and family counseling; but, never told, she did not know to ask. That was one of her first encounters with the unspoken culture of "if you don't ask, we won't tell" within the upper ranks.

Most of her supervisors were detached and very hands-off. Michelle felt alone and afraid. Away from family, friends, and her support network, she had no one in whom to confide.

Two years later a deployment opportunity arose for which Michelle volunteered. War was declared shortly into her tour of duty to Saudi Arabia, and her initial three-month separation from her husband turned into an extended eight months. Unlike her marriage, the military was there to stay. Michelle went on to serve active duty for a total of 12 years. Sadly, her marriage did not fare as well. Seven years in, she and her husband decided to go their separate ways.

San Antonio was home during her final years in the military. Michelle was in a new city, new job, going through a divorce. As if that were not bad enough, things at work took an unexpected turn for the worse. Her direct supervisor was a mature gentleman in his late sixties who worked civil service for over thirty years. She felt his approaches were often hard and unfair. It did not matter what she was doing or how well she was doing it, he patronized her in front of customers and peers alike. She went to the officer in charge to file a complaint, but nothing ever happened. There seemed to be no recourse.

Her next supervisor was different than what she had previously experienced, and it was a relief. He stressed to Michelle the importance of going to the clinic whenever something was wrong, physically, or emotionally. He was adamant about substantiating her work and how her performance needed to improve. He did what supervisors should: he supported his subordinates while allowing for autonomy. In other words, he led.

Upon his retirement, Michelle got a new supervisor who was dealing with personal challenges of her own. Reportedly, her manager's husband committed suicide in the very bed in which they slept each night. Michelle and others in her division thought the supervisor had come back too soon after her husband's death. As a result, she began taking her frustrations out on the staff, denying requests without explanation, and offering no job support. Michelle once again felt the familiar void of absent leadership. She was deprived of professional development opportunities and felt singled-out.

During her second year at Brooks AFB, under the 2005 Defense Appropriations Act, President Bush enacted a bill in which the military would be forced to decrease its footprint. This force-shaping reduction program had certain criteria Michelle met. She applied, and her application was accepted, so she could separate earlier than her original enlistment term. Michelle began the legwork for the actual discharge, a series of signatures that led to the production of military separation orders.

As soon as the application was approved, Michelle entered the Transition Assistance Program (TAP). She described the trainer as an older man who looked like he had stepped out of a bad 1980's film: scruffy sideburns, big toupee, wide-legged pants, and button down disco shirt underneath a top gun styled jacket (you know, knit waistband and sleeves rolled up to the elbow).

At the time, TAP was a three-day session. They spent part of the day talking about résumés which Michelle later described as antiquated. She was disappointed the program did not show her how to decipher military verbiage into civilian terms. Now, in the private sector for over ten years, she says, "Knowing how to translate military job functions into civilian terms would have made my résumé stronger and could have made all the difference in my employment opportunities."

TAP did not teach about salary negotiations nor did it reasonably explain how to translate military pay grade into civilian salaries. Michelle, like many, did not know what her military acquired skills were worth. Subsequently, the first position she accepted was below her warranted pay grade. We cover this most critical aspect of your transition in chapter six.

There were no classes that taught how to outfit, to wear a dress or skirt, or whether she should err on the side of caution and simply wear a pantsuit to her interviews. Michelle, like many, enlisted at a young age and subsequently spent a good part of her adulthood in the armed forces where uniforms were the required outfit, and ponytailed hair was apropos.

Michelle acknowledges she learned very little from the TAP. However, in a fortunate turn of events, when she transitioned to her second civilian job a year after her military separation, she was taught how to network, how to deliver an elevator speech, how to dress, and how to be successful, not only for the sake of the organization but herself.

The leadership team held each of their charges in high esteem. They mentored, advised, and remained far enough in the distance so each felt as if they were doing their job successfully on their own. They did what effective leaders must do: inspire confidence in those who look to them for direction. Commander James Stockdale, a highly-decorated officer and POW during the Vietnam war wrote, "Strange as it sounds, great leaders gain authority by giving it away." Not only did Michelle gain authority at the hands of her leaders, but she enjoyed her position immensely and subsequently earned a larger paycheck.

After Michelle separated from the military, the TAP underwent beneficial changes and updates. Per the Secretary of the Air Force, an AF Guidance Memorandum (AFGM) immediately modified AFI 36-3009 to institute Airman and Family Readiness Centers (AFRC). It implemented reforms to the processes of the Transition Assistance Program per Directive-type Memorandum (DTM) 12-007 "The implementation of Mandatory Transition Assistance Program Participation for Eligible Service Members."

The DTM bases its guidance and requirements on the Veteran Opportunity to Work Act (VOW Act) and the Veteran's Employment Initiative (VEI). Had those same initiatives been in place when Michelle separated, she may have met with a greater level of success at the onset of her civilian career.

Many men and women separate from the armed forces ill-prepared to face the rigors of a different way of life, succumbing to low-paying jobs, or unemployment, unable to translate valuable skills learned as servicemen to a successful, higher-paying civilian career.

As you can tell from Michelle's story, life in the military can have its difficulties, but for many of us, it is worthwhile. We are sworn in with hopes and dreams of a better future, of supporting, and being of service to our country. We gain valuable skills and a multitude of life-time benefits. We abandon all we know to be safe and secure for an uncertain and complicated way of life.

Like Michelle and David, many military families are torn apart by the very lifestyle afforded them as members of America's Armed Forces. Recurring deployments, relocations, mental illness, spousal separations, and single-parent households are among the many challenges facing our service members and their families every day.

Often, we get tested beyond our limits, but those same trials make us stronger and leave us better equipped to withstand life's unrelenting demands. Some of us separate with regrets, while others, like me, welcome a new way of life. Despite the challenges, we each have experiences and friendships that stay with us for a lifetime.

Unfortunate are those who end up with unbending leadership. Perhaps this is how the term "don't call me sir; I work for a living" got started. Most military personnel have either heard of or repeated the familiar phrase during their careers. It is a gentle jab at the officer corps "leadership" by the non-commissioned officer to distinguish rank earned through hard work and sacrifice versus rank obtained through academia, promotion, or appointment.

I am not saying the officer corps is not a crucial component of the military; I am highlighting the difference by which most enlisted people distinguish themselves.

Perhaps the main difference between the enlisted and officer, no matter the branch of service, is the enlisted are the crux of the US military with specialized training in both war and peacetime while the officers are managers over the enlisted, assigning tasks and giving various orders to follow. Both positions have roles important and necessary for the success of the mission.

It is my understanding that most NCOs take offense at being lumped in with an Officer. Though biased, my experience dealing with active duty and former military officers has shown me officer and enlisted each have the necessary skill set to lead and manage resources and teams. Both provide appropriate guidance to the enlisted to be proficient in his or her work.

Officers are not better than NCOs; their level of responsibility and accountability is different. As General Patton put it, "A leader is [simply] a man who can adapt principles to circumstances." Enlisted are trained from the onset to adapt. How well one acclimates is up to the individual.

Working as a civilian has been a wake-up call for me. Members of the armed forces take great pride in the high standards of military service. We hold others to our ideals and expect, somewhat naively, that they will adhere to the same standards of excellence.

The disciplined work ethic I adhered to while in the military is very different from expectations of me in the civilian workforce. Expectations once demanded of me by my superiors is now only self-imposed. I continue to observe the Air Force code of accountability and its standards of conduct and discipline, whether required or not. It serves me well in my position.

I often wonder if all civilian organizations should have a similar code of conduct and accountability. An individual's attitude would likely improve, workplace trivialities would decrease, and overall productivity would skyrocket. It would be an understatement to say there were never any issues in my varied military positions; but, when present, most were resolved quickly based on the individual's respect of the code of conduct. It was an expectation from which most of us did not stray too far.

To me, leadership demands an unspoken value system which benefits the whole and is not self-serving. Many civilian employees have the reputation of being narcissistic in nature. Those who climb the ladder tend to follow their agendas to the detriment of others. Often, managers are protecting their positions and damn be those under them.

I have witnessed this first hand; maybe you have too. Perhaps if there were a collective bargaining agreement at play, if the overall success of the company were equivalent to the good of the country as in the military, there would be less strife in the ranks. The "minions" might be less dissatisfied in the workplace if they felt their positions were as important as the upper levels. One major challenge for leadership is to make everyone in every area of the organization feel validated and appreciated while making a shared vision a reality.

I have been on both sides, military and civilian. I represent a host of employees who, like me, are self-compelled to serve at the highest capacity, no matter the role. As you read each account, you might see reflections of yourself in those featured in this book, including me. It is my hope you will use these experiences to help you successfully navigate your transitions, be they military, private, or significant life events.

Training, Commitment, and Core Values

When I was on active duty in the Air Force as a member of the Security Forces (Military Policeman), I enrolled in Airman Leadership School (ALS). Opportunely, ALS was my first official leadership course: five-weeks of intense Professional Military Education (PME), which strengthened my ability to lead, follow, and manage others.

That was also my earliest exposure to understanding what others' work duties were and how they related to mine. Just like the civilian's job description, each military professional has a Military Occupational Specialty code (MOS) or, as in my case, an Air Force Specialty Code (AFSC) that outlines job responsibilities.

This class was my first interactions with people whose job responsibilities differed from mine. Shortly into the class, I realized we were each working toward the same goal established by our command: to transition from Airmen into front-line supervisors. Everything we learned and practiced centered around leadership development, enhancing verbal and written communication skills, group dynamics, and the Profession of Arms.

All service men and women belong to the Profession of Arms, a code of conduct, set of core values, and commitment to meeting ethical and performance standards. Per *America's Air Force: A Profession of Arms "The Little Blue Book"[iv]* airmen, regardless of rank, share the common attributes of character, courage, and competence, qualifying as professionals through intensive training, education, and hands-on experience.

The United States Armed Forces' Core Values

Department of Defense (DOD)
Integrity, ethics, honor, courage, and loyalty

United States Army
Loyalty, duty, respect, selfless-service, honor, integrity, personal courage

United States Coast Guard
Honor, respect, and devotion to duty

The United States Marine Corps and US Navy
Honor, courage, and commitment

The United States Air Force
Integrity First, Service Before Self, and Excellence in all we do

The important traditions and culture of military life spill over into every aspect of civilian life. "Core Values provide a strong organizational identity. In addition, core values govern how people interact within the organization and guide the actions of individuals."[v] The various branches of service have not one philosophy that applies to all. Still, most members of the United States Armed Forces operate with the highest ethics, courage, commitment, and honor of any who have ever lived.

These ideologies are not exclusive to military personnel. The policeman, firefighter, paramedic, and other civil servants live by values that drive their behaviors, understanding how it looks and feels to embody discipline, courage, honor, loyalty, duty, integrity, and endurance. The following stories illustrate those ideals.

My friend's father retired in 2006 as a decorated chief officer with the Fire Department of a mid-sized northeastern city. He began his career as a tillerman, steering the rear of firetrucks through rain, snow, sleet, and hail.

At fires, his job venting roofs on multifamily homes and high-rises was extremely dangerous. Wearing up to seventy-five pounds of Personal Protection Equipment (PPE) or turnout gear only added to the hazard. A certain amount of dexterity was necessary just to walk! Nevertheless, every day the call of duty propelled him to execute assignments to the best of his ability because lives were at stake. His occupation demanded he risk his life to save others.

The National Firefighter Code of Ethics encourages fire service personnel to promote a culture of ethical integrity and high standards of professionalism in their field.[vi] These ethics dictate members exercise professionalism, competence, respect, and loyalty while upholding the duties that benefit and protect those to whom they serve.

Firefighters are mandated to govern themselves with high moral standards. They are to conduct themselves, on and off duty, in a manner reflecting positively on their department and the fire service in general. These too are the universal traits setting apart members of the armed forces from others.

We saw this inspired call to arms in response to the September 11th attacks on the World Trade Centers. Thousands of firefighters, without pause, risked, and many ultimately lost their lives adhering to a code of ethics to which many of us will never be exposed. Of the nearly 3000 fatalities, a combined 411 emergency responders were killed, of whom over 340 were firefighters.[vii]

There were several communications difficulties during the rescue efforts. Due to the sporadic reception from the portable radios used during recovery efforts, the chief officers never knew if their messages got through to the rescue units. Even so, responders continued their valiant attempts to evacuate and save lives, despite faulty radio transmissions from command central.

Efforts to improve flawed communications failed because numerous firefighters could not receive messages under the collapsed building rubble.

Those brave men and women risked life and limb because of the code of ethics to which they adhered. They were no less leaders than the chief officers commanding the rescue operations.

Although my friend's father never experienced a disaster as horrific as 9/11, he did honor his call to duty by performing at a level akin to a respected leader and hero.

"Any man's death diminishes me, because I am involved in mankind; and therefore, never send to know for whom the bell tolls; it tolls for thee."
John Donne

Throughout his career, he rose from private to lieutenant, captain to battalion chief to acting deputy chief. His ascent up the ranks was the result of discipline and hard work. He spent hundreds of hours studying so he could score high enough on the Department's promotional exams to one day realize his goals of advancement.

Even with his remarkable achievements, his greatest accomplishment was, while still a private, saving the life of a fellow firefighter while battling an inferno. For his act of bravery, he received the Fire Department's second highest award, the Medal of Valor. Various community organizations honored him. He received proclamations and citations from city and state officials and won the admiration of his peers and superiors alike.

I share these examples if only to illustrate that leadership qualities are no respecter of position, rank, grade, age, or class. When you are self-motivated to excel, you do so while in any position, even under the worse of conditions. You do not need or wait for permission to stand tall and respond when duty summons. We call these model, self-possessed personality types "High Speed, Low Drag." The admirable qualities defining leaders are self-prescribed.

One such attribute is the ability to take charge while also being led. A real leader understands well that he or she must uphold a deeply held code of conduct even when under attack. He must communicate those values by first standing as an example, and ultimately, by demanding it of those he leads.

As the events of 9/11 have shown us, effective communication can make an organization or operation just as ineffective communication can break one. However, in the absence of direction, it is up to the individual to chart his or her best course of action.

Imagine the first responders and many others on September 11, 2001, whose lives were saved not because of the commands of their department chiefs, but because they were self-directed in their darkest hour. Perhaps fate spared their lives. We might never know. What we do know is the men and women who did not survive, died in courageous service to their country that day, and thousands of survivors returned home safely to their families.

Those brave men and women are American heroes. Every responder lived up to his and her pledge to serve, honor, and protect. The words "service before self," for all who swear an oath of office, describe an unbreakable bond with another regardless of background or beliefs.

These are not just any words; rather, they represent a shared philosophy and responsibility to society—an internal Brotherhood. Core values are what connects each branch of service to the next, and ultimately to the world. It is, in my opinion, a precursor to all other leadership initiatives undertaken by any serviceman or woman.

☆ ☆ ☆ ☆ ☆

The second formal training I participated in was the Noncommissioned Officer Academy (NCOA). This six-week course prepares NCOs to be professionals who can lead and manage Air Force units with the goal of developing Airmen into effective *mid-level* leaders and managers.

During class, it was important for us to share among each other ideas, experiences, and perspectives to increase our proficiency in all areas of command. I gained greater insights into what it takes to lead and communicate on a higher organizational level. I also realized how important effective communication is to an organization. Just like the chief command of the 9/11 operations, without effective communication, life and death directives may be deemed useless.

The next eight-week class was the Senior Non-Commissioned Officer Academy (SNCOA) which is an advanced military education program designed to foster greater leadership responsibilities in select NCOs. The curriculum centers on the understanding that elite men and women already bring to the table a high level of competency.

Those of you who have undertaken these programs know each development opportunity, spaced a few years apart, ensure we receive the necessary training at precisely the right time in our careers. There is a focus on national security objectives, organizational, behavioral, and advanced leadership skills on a functional, operational, and strategic level. These courses also allow for an increased level of understanding and comradery with our peers.

Military members undertake rigorous training initiatives, but most employers underestimate the vast transferable skills we possess. Many who enjoy a breadth of responsibility in their military positions end up with civilian jobs that do not take full advantage of their expertise. They work in positions with insufficient opportunities to demonstrate their skills and abilities.

I find private enterprises are in the dark when it comes to the demands of these strategically placed training advancements and how they provide professional growth opportunities.

Whether officer or enlisted, one thing is for sure, *all* have a skill set capable of benefiting any company or organization. We have unsurpassed problem-solving acuity, cognitive skills, strategic thinking acumen, and a strong grasp of business management concepts. We train as part of our promotional eligibility and as a rite of passage among ourselves.

Perhaps our training and commitment makes us adhere to a higher standard of conduct than our civilian counterparts. This training is willfully directed by the Uniform Code of Military Justice (UCMJ), an enactment of Congress that establishes the foundation of laws for U.S. military services. It is mandatory.

The military professional learns from day one in basic training, if they are the person with the most rank and or authority in each situation, they will be the one to take charge.

I attended my inaugural leadership and management course when I was 22 years old, followed by my next course a few years later, with subsequent classes spaced a few years apart throughout my time spent in service. My first supervisor told me I would one day manage, lead, and eventually take his place. He masterfully developed an individualized learning path for me to follow and set very clear expectations of how I should proceed.

This knowledge did not come without its stripes. I was faced with a set of unique, albeit embarrassing tests like the one my supervisor administered when teaching me how to operate a HUMVEE. During a training exercise as a rookie military police officer, my supervisor yelled, "Go start the vehicle and get me the damn HUMVEE keys—right now!" I rushed off frantically, searching high and low for the keys but to no avail. For those of you who may not already know, a HUMVEE does not require a key to start.

That was one of more embarrassing, yet impactful supervisory moments passed down from superior to a subordinate, and I taught my subordinates likewise. I viewed my supervisor as a hard ass, but it was moments like these that made him human. Because I no longer saw him as larger than life, but as a human being (with a sense of humor I might add) I followed his lead. I was already motivated to succeed, but his direction was certainly memorable in my quest for gaining a heightened sense of confidence.

I supervised 16 people immediately following initial professional development course. My professional duties and responsibilities only grew from there. Surprisingly, I never felt I was alone in my decision-making duties as a front-line leader. Even if I failed to seek assistance from my assigned supervisor, I always knew guidance and counseling was available to me from my superiors.

As for my civilian career, I sometimes struggle identifying those leaders with whom I can have a similar rapport and relationship. There is a big difference in the way military supervisors approach a commitment of accountability versus the typical civilian response to their subordinate's job advancement.

While working at my first post-military job, I remember asking my supervisor, "Who is responsible for a subordinate's development?" He lashed out, "You are responsible for your professional development! It's my job to guide you along your journey." Effective leaders must allow others to stand on their own, but they must also put in place the means for an individual to do so. Most past and present military supervisors will tell you they believe the subordinate's development is a direct reflection of the leader's ability to lead.

Understand, as Michelle experienced, there are weak leaders in the military just as there are unmotivated workers in each sector. Leaders, whether in government or corporate America, are supposed to ensure those under their watch excel in their positions and elevate themselves through personal and professional development.

I recently had the opportunity to speak before an audience at the local state university. I was elated to learn that a few of the Masters of Business Administration (MBA) students worked at the same company as me. The candid discussions about the lack of professional development existing in my organization were astounding!

The conversation centered around one gentleman in the class who had landed a new position with a higher pay rate. He explained how the organization promoted him through natural attrition. He was advancing not because he was a star performer (his words) but merely because his boss was leaving the company and he, MBA degree in hand, was next in line to replace him.

This recently promoted individual felt the company provided no leadership development training to help him in his new role; and, because of that, he was unsure if he was going to accept the promotion.

The reason his story hits so close to home is my experience in the military has taught me that there are clear delineations and expectations one must meet in both training and experience-based requirements before one qualifies for a promotion. This type of professional development is laid out for every individual in a concise way so he or she can understand the various pathways to success.

This young man, although a great promotional opportunity lay before him, felt unprepared for his next leadership role. JFK perhaps knew best when he reminded us, "Leadership and learning are indispensable to each other." To me, failure to prepare him for promotion was a severe organizational leadership failure. Had he (as should other employees) been given a structured approach that allowed for professional development in every position and rank, he might have looked forward to his new role.

I was fortunate. Many of my civilian friends never achieve the level of accountability and responsibility during their entire working career I gained at such a young age. Was I ready for this level of responsibility at the time? I did not have a choice. The first six weeks in the military I had been encouraged to grab the responsibility baton when it was handed off to me.

Truth told, the onus was always mine, only I did not know it at the time. But, it was not long before I was ready to stand tall at the tip of the spear. Henry Ford once said, "You don't have to hold a position in order to be a leader." My early experiences in the Air Force proved that correct.

The military quickly taught me how to lead with dignity, strength, and a sense of purpose far exceeding my expectations. Few managers in civilian organizations have been subjected to the same level of intense leadership training and experience as I was as an airman. This invaluable skill set armed me with the ability to address organizational challenges head-on; granted this gift can be a curse depending on who is telling the story.

For one, military members have experienced the world through a different lens. We prepare at the highest level for the threat of war, terrorism, and homeland security. The unyielding demands of life as members of the armed forces place us in a unique position many unfamiliar with the military will ever comprehend.

Do not expect others to understand, yet be cognizant of sharing your experiences with those around you so they may benefit from your example. Nobel Peace Prize recipient Albert Schweitzer said, "Example is not the main thing in influencing others, it is the only thing." Refrain from sharing all your "war stories," but do work on connecting your diverse experiences with your civilian co-workers so their capabilities can develop because of your strengths.

Throughout my years in the military and civilian sector I have encountered men and women whose very strengths separate them from the pact. It is becoming increasingly apparent to me that position, stature, nor college degree make you a real leader. Having the ability to direct others is far more involved than a title; it takes un-matched talents and skills not manufactured, taught, or bought.

I can tell you, however, when you show high levels of self-awareness, competence, humility, and emotional intelligence—traits of those who not only meet the challenge of leadership but surpass it—you are supported in your efforts.

Some people have difficulty managing themselves, never mind others. Not everyone will heed the call to lead. You may know of professionals who, in positions of authority, wield an uncompromising sword in the workplace, in their personal lives, and homes. What does that tell you about a person? What does it say about his leadership style? If nothing else, you could say he is consistent. Leadership demands constancy.

Too often, managers waver in their roles, allowing favoritism and personal biases to pollute their interactions with subordinates, undermining the very position they are paid to manage.

I have known and continue to meet people who claim to be the greatest leader and manager under the sun, only to be proven unworthy of the title. Experience has taught me to view those in authority with discernment. Like me, you might know of or have known those persons who are in positions where the question begs asking, "How the hell did they ever get there?"

☆☆☆☆☆

The Takeaway

Motivational Speaker Brian Tracy asks us to "become the kind of leader that people would follow voluntarily; even if you had no title or position." Remember, we each must follow to the letter a code of conduct under every circumstance. We must remain self-directed in our actions and demonstrate in ourselves what we hope to see in others. Above all, integrity must be front and center in every thought and interaction. Integrity is the cornerstone of leadership, the barometer of character, and the foundation of all other traits.

CHAPTER TWO

PLANNING TO PIVOT

"If you
are going to achieve
excellence in big things, you
develop the habit in little things. Excellence
is not an exception; it is a prevailing attitude."
Colin Powell

I retired from the military after 21 years of active duty service. The US Air Force makes available for its separating members several useful programs. I found the Transition Assistance Programs (TAP) to be lacking, but I did receive a few helpful tips that helped me problem solve and come up with different solutions. Although the bulk of this program lasted a full day, it was better than some received when released from duty after Vietnam and Desert Storm.

One of my more seasoned friends, Walter, served in the Marine Corps Reserve after receiving his undergraduate degree. He trained at the esteemed Marine Corps Base Quantico for six months before going to Camp Lejeune in Jacksonville, North Carolina. From there he was deployed to the Republic of Vietnam. In 1972, a cease-fire agreement was signed, but not implemented. Three years later Saigon fell to communist forces.

Through the ravages of a punishing war, Walter returned to US soil. Still, killed in action in Vietnam was an estimated 60,000 American servicemen and women, with another 150,000 wounded.[viii] Because he had served on active duty for more than 180 days between February 28, 1961, and May 7, 1975, Walter was eligible to separate after 13 months of service defending his country under the American troop's reduction "Vietnamization" program.

After an honorable discharge, Walter found himself unemployed, reflecting on what he would do next. He spent many sleepless nights weighing his options until finally deciding to attend a job fair in Jacksonville. Visiting with different companies at the fair afforded him the opportunity to speak face to face with those in charge of hiring. His confidence and character stood out to a staffing manager with one of the attending companies.

Two weeks later Walter was invited to Ohio for an interview which resulted in a lengthy and rewarding career with Metro Health Medical Center in Cleveland. He eventually became a VP of Human Resources, responsible for over six thousand employees.

Walter went on to receive his master's degree from Case Western University. He credits his time in officer training school with preparing him to be an effective leader and communicator. War, however, readied him for experiences he hopes never to relive, but which served him well in his leadership role.

Without the benefit of a transition assistance program, Walter had to navigate his transition alone. In fact, because the Vietnam war was so controversial, many of our nation's fighters who returned seemingly unaffected by the ravages of combat, kept their experiences to themselves.

Others, outwardly affected by the brutality and carnage of an unconscionable war, overloaded the VA system. Vietnam War veterans suffered PTSD, labeled as such in 1980.[ix] As a side note, during World War I veterans endured what was called "shell-shock" and later given the treatment name of "war neuroses." World War II veterans experienced Battle Fatigue, later classified as Combat Stress Reaction (CSR).

Stories throughout history have made known disenfranchised men and women who, for many decades, sacrificed their lives only to be cast aside as irreparably damaged. I share Walter's account with you to show not all troops relied on assistance to launch successful careers. Many are self-inclined to do what they must do.

> "Even if a person has only served one minute of one hour of one day in any branch of the Armed Forces, they will always have my eternal respect and heartfelt gratitude."

American soldiers of World Wars I and II often returned home to a show of pageantry: red carpet laid out, received as heroes in the broadest sense of the word, with numerous job offers to consider. Walter, and tens of thousands like him, returned from Vietnam to a divided, post-segregationist America. Civil and women's rights shone brightly, up close and personal in our nation's consciousness. Illicit drug use was rampant, and the government was failing her people. Little did Walter know the comradery he found in combat would remain buried in the jungles of Viet Cong.

What separates a Walter from those men and women who are unable to transition, or pivot successfully? To recognize this, you must first understand what a pivot is.

Steve Blank, himself a Vietnam veteran and arguably one of the country's top authorities on the lean startup, suggests a pivot requires you to substantially change components of a business model or, the various parts of your company's strategy to arrive at different outcomes.[x] So, if we look at your transition plan as the "product" and the several phases of your plan as the "strategy," we would, in pivoting, evaluate which measures are working and which are not. We would take those steps and products yielding little to no results (like my résumé which we will touch on soon), mindfully rework or discard them, and replace them with something more efficient.

While I, nor any of my contemporaries have served in Vietnam, we stand on the shoulders, to an extent, of brothers and sisters lost in combat generations before us. Like Walter, whether we served on the front line or sat behind a desk, we are equally yoked and prepared for battle and yes, death.

When our service is complete, we, unlike the men and women of early to mid-twentieth-century wars can receive help, no matter how flawed, from a multitude of federal assistance programs. Nonetheless, the disappointing advice I received from the TAP was not nearly enough for me to seamlessly transition from what I had known for over 20 years.

One of the ways in which the program helped me with my transition was through the *"just keep asking yourself the appropriate questions"* approach. This tactic was simply a litany of questions I was to think about and provide answers to, like the 5-why interrogative technique (a pseudo one-man brainstorming session). Its goal is to determine the cause of a problem by repeating the "why?" until you strip away the number of iterations needed to solve the problem. It is a useful experiment in persistence if nothing else. The trouble was, I already had enough damn questions of my own! What I needed was to be pointed in the right direction. It was hard to find answers to my "whys" through a couple of seminars that made up the TAP.

Transition assistance programs, many of which are mandated by Congress, are to prepare service members and their families for a successful changeover to civilian life. Each military branch has a TAP, offering the same or comparable benefits and services, and each has notable similarities in their ineffectiveness.

Regardless of the branch of service, the programs are supposed to provide pre-separation counseling, workshops, numerous briefings designed to help you better navigate the multifarious VA system, and overall transitioning support.

Federal law requires the service branches to verify military experience and training of transitioning service members. The Verification of Military Experience and Training (VMET) DD Form 2586 summarizes this material, shows recommended college credit information, and suggests civilian equivalent job titles.[xi] This step in the transitioning process could prove to be highly beneficial to the separating veteran.

Just before I retired, the Air Force had two types of TAP programs comprised of one, two, and three-day seminars. When I entered the programs, former senior enlisted personnel ran them, intermingled with a few former senior officers, and a sprinkle of civilians. At the time, the program looked and sounded good to me.

Initially, I viewed the workshops, together with the overwhelming diversity of the staff administering them, as a recipe for success.

It did not take long before I was disillusioned. The counselors offered little more than I already knew. All said, the program, for me, was virtually a waste of time. The one good thing I got out of the TAP was it forced me to ask *better* questions, not only to the staff but of myself.

One of the issues I had both then and now is: "Why are the recently transitioned officers and enlisted working this 'pit stop?' Were the officers there because they inadequately prepared for their own separations? Did they have a problem letting go of an airmen's way of life? Did they continue to yearn for the solidarity found in the military?"

As one can imagine, the military has a very high turnover rate due to national security needs, attrition, Permanent Change of Station (PCS), contingency operational requirements, injury, discharges, retirement, and death. Because the transition assistance office was also known to have a high turnover rate, one might presume these positions were used to assist former senior staff in their professional evolutions.

Whatever the case, I was told only what I already knew: I must rely on my thinking, planning, and goal-setting to have a successful transition. What I needed, and therefore what I was hoping to get from the TAP, was definitive answers to not only the "whys" but the "who, what, when, and how" of successful transitions.

I had become accustomed to having direction. Now, to whom do I turn? What was I supposed to do? What type of position should I look for in my job search? How and when do I search for a job, especially after transitioning to civilian status from an overseas location? Was I going about it the right way? What is a résumé and why do I need one? Will a company pay for housing and clothing? Does the organization offer health insurance? And the big one: what am I worth? I am sure you will have plenty of questions of your own which I hope to answer.

I found it then, as I sometimes do now, problematic to translate into civilian terms the wide-ranging skills I acquired in my military career. Just as Michelle articulated in the previous chapter, we are not offered tutorials on this translation for a variety of reasons.

The "professional assistance" was presented by individuals who seemed motivated but who had recently separated themselves, and did not have the training or expertise to give me the guidance I sought. They did not offer enough answers to satisfy my thirst to know more about the transition process.

Some of the employees in the TAP had insufficient corporate experience so I was referred to civilian-based paid services and useless advisory books to bridge the relentless preparation gap. In hindsight, I would not know what I do know if it had not been for my determination to gather as much information as possible to help me in my transition.

Unfortunately, countless service members and I got directed to the savage multi-billion-dollar career assistance, employment, and job placement industry. I say "savage" because the industry has (in my opinion) many fraudulent services of which veterans get conned out of a lot of hard earned money.

I will reiterate this in a later chapter, but you should not be paying out-of-pocket for government-based transition assistance. Many federal agencies and programs rely on external services, or "partner organizations." These cohorts are usually for-profit companies that do not necessarily have your best interests at heart. Their bottom-line comes first.

The Employment & Recruiting Agencies Industry is huge. Per IBISWorld, this massive industry includes companies listing employment vacancies and other employment-related services. These establishments have a combined annual revenue of over twenty-seven billion dollars.[xii] You read correctly, twenty-seven billion! Those companies make a whole lot of dough off the backs of the soon to be separated military professionals!

Industry products include executive search firms, employment agencies, casting agencies, HR consulting firms, permanent placement services, and others. I am all for free enterprise, but many of the services for which these companies charge, TAP is supposed to offer its separated members for free! Therefore, why pay for an entitlement for which we sacrificed our lives to earn?

One of the many myths I uncovered while figuring out my post-military life was these agencies assist you in your civilian job search and help prepare you for life after the military. I found that to be far from the truth.

Throughout most of my career, I was told stories about the "outside" as if separating from the military was equivalent to being released from prison.

On top of not knowing what to do, a slew of misinformation circulated about the transition from a military to a civilian career. There is a whole lot of BS floating in the ether, waiting patiently for an unsuspecting mind to fall for the hype.

Another myth you may encounter is that you will return stateside to the applause of a waiting crowd and given the key to the city. I am exaggerating of course, but you get the gist. While this type of reception is happening less and less, I vividly recall when I first returned from a deployment while in the Desert Shield campaign.

My first port of entry was Bangor Maine. When I, along with other members of the 4th Security Police Squadron arrived, a few dozen older women were there waiting to welcome us with music, open arms, and a feeling of heroism incredibly uplifting.

My daughters use to meet me at the airport after my deployments and Temporary Duty Assignments (TDY) to which their screams of "Daddy, daddy, welcome home!" could only be held as second to their smiling faces and tight hugs around the neck. How I cherish those precious memories. Returning military members transitioning to the civilian sector should not expect this type of welcome at their new civilian workplace. It happens, but it is rare.

TRANSITIONING MYTHS

Myth #1 There is no money out there. This I proved to be false; I initially found a job making almost $25,000 more a year than I made at the height of my active duty career.

Myth #2 No job will give you the satisfaction like working for the military. While this was certainly true for me, working as a civilian has been a different kind of satisfaction thus far.

Myth #3 You will get your "freedom" back when you get in "the real world." Wait, you mean I can quit my job if I want? I had visions of finding a job just so I could experience quitting a position.

Myth #4 You will not be deployed so you will have more time with your family. Depending on the position you land, this can be grossly untrue.

Myth #5 The corporate structure is sometimes undisciplined and not focused on the right things. While this may not be true in all businesses, I felt this *was* true at my organization.

Myth #6 Civilians do not know how to work together as a team. Outcomes on this one vary; *see your nearest highly reliable organization for further details.*

Despite the myths, getting my first civilian job was one of the hardest things I had to do after my transition. Nevertheless, I was successful because I had a system with quantifiable steps, focused execution, and lots of hustle every day. In the next section, we will delve further into the methodology I used. As you read further, understand I spent a considerable amount of time before my separation preparing for my departure. You must too.

As I began my transition to the civilian workforce, I found it difficult to focus on the task at hand while finding that sweet spot between mission execution and at last being able to concentrate on myself as a civilian. I had an idea of what I might face, so I got started long before my final year of service. I made useful contacts early.

The sooner you begin exploring companies, employment agencies or headhunters, the sooner you will receive help with your career transition. Starting your employment search early builds knowledge of the job market and puts your name in front of people who can help you. It also affords you a better understanding of the necessary steps to successfully land a job that best utilizes your skills, talents, and personality.

Identifying Skills and Abilities

Military-based support services personnel suggest you take a Myers-Briggs Type Indicator® (MBTI®) to understand what your interests and strengths are to determine appropriate job matches. The purpose of the personality inventory is to make the theory of psychological types described by C. G. Jung understandable and useful in people's lives.[xiii] The concept is that random variations in behavior are orderly and consistent. I agree; you must vary your mindset and practices to suit the current situation.

As most military members know, when facing do or die extremes, gut instinct has a way of kicking in and winning over. These "hunches" will help during your job search and are always consistent. Learn to trust yours.

These placement tests and services sell with the understanding a person's job search will be more productive. Many of the assessments are psychology-based and are supposed to shed light on your personality type and how well you relate to others. These evaluations may be beneficial, but I found them skewed because baseline criteria focused on civilian experiences, not military acquired skills.

We already know how we relate to others; day in and day out, we work with, fight alongside, and protect one another. We eat, sleep, laugh, and cry next to our military brothers and sisters. We charge into battle with men and women of different stripes and vastly disparate socio-economic backgrounds. We must relate to our comrades; live are at stake.

Anyway, the price point of these services ranged from $50-800 per person. You might need them; I do not know. You are reading this book, so I can only surmise that maybe you need direction like I once did. Only you can decide whether the tests (or this book) will be beneficial to you in your job search. I was determined to prepare as best I could—given the lack of guidance—which is why I spent days on end structuring my transition. Once I could translate my skill set and relate it better to the organization's needs, I had something in which companies were greatly interested.

In the military, I learned I could achieve far more than any aptitude test might predict. These tests are based on a person's overall experience and serve as a forecast into his or her future capabilities. And yet, I have never bought into the notion that your yesterday determines your tomorrow.

I see myself perfectly capable of envisioning and creating a prosperous future, despite prior successes or failures. Franklin D. Roosevelt once said, "The only limit to our realization of tomorrow will be our doubts of today." Therefore, be single-minded, in the moment. Do not gaze over your shoulder into the past, regretting what you did or did not do.

Yesterday is gone. The only do-over you get is to wake each day determined to accomplish what you can in the 24-hours you are [hopefully] given. Make real-time, command decisions that lead to the fulfillment of both strategic and tactical objectives with the operational precision demanded of US service members. Learn what you can, when you can, and put every piece of information to good use. So, if knowledge is power, get ready to become a god.

The Steward Methodology

1. I took a thorough inventory of my skills and talents, strengths, weaknesses, likes and dislikes. You must be completely honest with yourself when doing this first step. Now is the time to face the man in the mirror. Business magnate Warren Buffett said, "Defining your circle of competence is the most important aspect of investing." You, in fact, are investing in yourself, and must also "set your circle of expertise."

2. I scoured online employment sites and listed types of positions for which I was best suited based on a combination of my skills self-assessment and relevant job postings. A good place to check out is USAjobs.gov, which has a list of positions and their requirements.

3. I narrowed down the number of companies and industries to whom I could best contribute based on my aptitude and personality. This step is critical for obtaining a good match and is a similar formula used by job placement services.

4. I researched the specifics of the civilian position and general salary range and compared it to my current military pay grade.

5. I compiled data in chronologic and historical order to tell the story of my specific accomplishments during my military career. Here you will want to be as detailed as possible using numbers and percentages to highlight a progression of successes.

6.   I gathered all my past enlisted performance reports (EPR) and completed a SWOT Analysis (strengths, weaknesses, opportunities, and threats) to weigh the specific characteristics my managers identified in me. Do not stop there; follow up this technique by completing a TOWS table to brainstorm specific strategies, matching your "threats to your opportunities and your weaknesses with your strengths."

7.   I compiled a comprehensive list of my major strengths. This list allowed me to analyze my abilities in ways beneficial to a civilian employer: being team-oriented, working well under pressure individually and within a group, dedication to something bigger than myself, etc. I continually work on my weaknesses as an ongoing exercise in becoming my best. Internationally acclaimed motivational speaker and writer Jim Rohn wrote, "Successful people do what unsuccessful people are not willing to do. Do not wish it were easier, wish you were better."

8.   I researched civilian job titles that matched my career interests, played to my strengths, and offered the best career path.

9.   I looked at and compared (after much trial and error) industry standard verbiage the job postings used and ensured my résumé contained the same or similar phrasing and keywords. This one step alone will likely increase your chance of your résumé getting past skimming software and reviewed by a human. *(we'll get to that later)*

10. I found out the names of recruiters, head hunters, hiring managers, and Human Resource directors, and I addressed my correspondence to a person, not a "to whom it may concern."

And, although I do not include this final suggestion in my methodology, I want you to give it thought: wherever an employment opportunity presents, consider it. That could mean moving to an unfamiliar area. Remember, Walter transferred to another state and enjoyed a long, rewarding career. I landed in a locale almost two thousand miles from where I grew up and could not be happier.

You might contemplate relocating overseas (contracting positions abroad may pay considerably more). It may well mean separating from your family for a short time after you accept a position and go through a required probationary period. Weigh all options.

If a job appeals to you and covers everything in your self-assessment, do not hesitate to venture outside of your comfort zone. Author Neale Donald Walsch tells us: "Life begins at the end of your comfort zone." In other words, do not be afraid to try new things.

The military has a way, despite the hazards, of giving us a [pseudo] sense of well-being. Our needs are met, we have armed security surrounding us 24-7, and we adopt our wartime brothers and sisters as family. We figure out how to live and adapt within this protective lair. It is sometimes hard to adjust outside of that cocoon. Nevertheless, reflect carefully on the relocation facet of your transition. It might prove to be one of the best decisions of your life.

Attention to Orders

Employers do not want to hear what you want but rather how you can help make their organizational vision become a reality. For the employer, it is a cost vs. value proposition. Simply put, the more you can bring to the table, the higher you will be valued. Most of the companies I encountered shared with me what they look for in new recruits. If you can answer the who, what, when, why, and how of what is wanted, you will have one leg up on the competition. Use the following criteria as a benchmark:

1. Hiring agents highly recommend individuals who are focused and single-minded; those who know what they want, how to achieve it, and how it might benefit the organization. Then, perceived as goal-oriented (which is a key factor in personal marketability) you will be one step ahead of others rivaling for the same position.

2. The ability to articulate your unique qualifications and how you not only relate to the whole but how you interact within the whole, will serve you well. If you are not a team player, it does not matter one iota what you bring to the table.

3. The answer to why you want to be employed by an organization is possibly the greatest selling tool military members possess. We have lived the mandate of service

before self, and thus rewarded in unique ways for taking part in something greater than ourselves. If you can passionately convey that sentiment to an interviewer or recruiter, and how it relates to the company's philosophy (and bottom-line), bravo!

The reality is, it is tough for the transitioning veteran to look qualified in the eyes of an employer. Companies are looking for "specific industry experience," and unfortunately, there are those in charge who do not see military experience (even in related fields) as relevant.

The obstacle becomes relating your unique set of experiences to what the employers' needs are. If you can communicate those experiences and how advantageous they are to the company, you are golden. Remember, with my first position as a civilian I made nearly twenty-five thousand dollars per year more than my highest pay grade while enlisted and it has only gone up from there. Establishing your income threshold at the onset of your search will do wonders for future salary negotiations.

Considered a post-military success, the values I adopted while enlisted did not always align with my changing world view. Selfless sacrifice, for instance, was not quite as important to me as finding personal meaning, satisfaction and prioritizing my family. What ways have your values changed since you left the Armed Forces? My values did not change, but my priorities shifted. Another pivot, therefore, was in order.

Instead of service before self, (AF Core Value) now it is family first, despite what external duties demand of me. I do not put my civilian job first because we are not at war and we do not provide brothers on the ground with supplies or close air support. I put my family first by refusing overtime, night shift or weekends. I held a high sense of loyalty to my mission while enlisted, but I do not embrace the same level of devotion to my employer.

This allegiance shows how having a positive attitude, and brave heart can help a person overcome difficult times. "An open and receptive intellect permits a leader to challenge existing assumptions about his environment and generate new ways of thinking as a means of adjusting to a new environment. This is an intellectual achievement of the first order and characterizes the thinking of history's great commanders."[xiv]

A civilian may have the same experiences and show similar credentials as the former military with perhaps one exception: civilians cannot always prove their work experiences translate to the same historical events to which former military people were exposed.

This is not to say civilians do not have life-changing events in their history which can prove useful in the workplace. It is only to say that war, and the threat of war establishes an emotional and intellectual dexterity most employers would be prudent to recognize. Increasingly, leadership "experts" are finally acknowledging that experience and more recently, emotional intelligence, trumps book knowledge in almost every circumstance of corporate governance and daily living.

☆☆☆☆☆

The military is not made up of people who look exactly like me, act as I do, or share the same beliefs as me. Over the course of my career, I have worked with, followed, managed, and led diverse groups of individuals. I have attained a global perspective on how to effectively interact with different races, cultures, genders, and ages.

The United States Air Force instilled in me an ability to work as one team focused on one mission. I now know myself better and what I can capably accomplish.

Still, after my separation from the military, at my first job I was as uneasy as a kindergartener on his first day of school. I had not yet considered how my abilities aligned with civilian dictates. For those military-related skills, I was still uncertain how to translate them to civilian market demands.

Do not get me wrong, if I were a sniper with the 10th Mountain Division, I would not put on a résumé "successfully eliminated 250 targets while I was deployed in Afghanistan" if trying to get a job at the post office. But, I could say I have a heightened sense of awareness of my surroundings and perform well in a team to ensure operational success. The former military has many competencies that could place any organization at an advantage. The proper translation of those skills will assist you in outlining your résumé and help you during the interview process.

When interpreting these gained skills, the journey is like the anxiety and difficulty a person has learning a new language. You must slow down and shut off your internal dialogue, listen, and think of how to translate one form of speech to another. Similarly, we must convert military specific tasks into their civilian equivalent. Let us now look at a few of those deciphered skills:

Military Police

- Leadership skills
- Physical and mental toughness
- Training in law enforcement
- Weaponry knowledge
- Respect for the law
- Heightened sense of awareness

Engineering Technician

- Assist higher-graded technicians and engineers
- Ability to process complex data
- Surveying and testing equipment
- Conduct survey work
- Retrieves pertinent information from many sources
- Knowledgeable of construction plans and specifications
- Ensures deliverables meet quality control

Contract Specialist-Finance

- Performs market research/analysis
- Analyzes market trends and commercial practices
- Selects contracting approaches, techniques & procedures
- Performs acquisition planning
- Uses judgment interpreting guidelines
- Determines actions on assigned contracts

- Provides business advice & assistance to technical personnel
- Reviews requisition packages for adequacy & compliance

The list could go on and on. I gleaned these examples from a job database at USAjobs.gov. They lay out for you the wide-ranging duties and qualifications of each position. It is important to utilize sites like this one when compiling tasks and responsibilities for your résumé. Take your current job description and match it word for word; it contains a goldmine of keywords and phrases.

During my civilian job search, I discovered that larger companies review and filter résumés using talent management and applicant tracking software. This software program hones in on keywords and phrases, matching the job posting as advertised. I did not know what all of this meant but soon realized if I did not have a certain percentage of these words or phrases in my résumé, I stood no chance of even getting past the picking phase.

Case in point: a job posting might feature a company looking for a candidate with a graduate degree and at least five years of experience at the mid-management level. Hence, the software is programmed to look for just that: a candidate with a graduate degree who has at least five years of mid-management experience. If you cannot see the potential conflict with this approach, you will remain one in a pool of candidates.

Job hunters sweat over their résumés, sometimes spending hundreds of dollars to produce what will hopefully be a winner, only to have it go sight unseen by human eyes.

Additionally, one completes the application screening online. You might spend an hour or more answering a barrage of questions that determine your "personality type." Combining the information in your profile with details in your application and suddenly an employer knows everything about you. The following statement is what I was told, almost verbatim, from my first résumé submission:

"Roderick Steward's experience appears to be concentrated in engineering with exposure to knowledge and learning management. Roderick Steward has 21 years of work experience, with little to no management experience. WARNING: The candidate's primary skill appears to be in engineering, but the job objective seems to show interest in a different area." My current résumé did not stand a chance to beat the system. I had to change my approach. So, I retooled my résumé and started from square one.

This "scratch and sniff" method does not consider candidates who meet the *minimum* education requirements with 20 years of global strategic experience. A computer's methodology is void of the human factor. The software's algorithms bypassed the aggressive management and supervision duties embedded in my résumé because I did not use the right "buzzwords."

Most software programs "skim" for skills which match a narrow range of key concepts from the job description. If you do not know the specific words and phrases to use, you are out of luck; your résumé will not make the cut.

Regrettably, many qualified candidates are often overlooked based on this system. My résumé, as first written, stood no chance at getting past the computer program and on to one who would read it.

So, what can one do? You recalibrate and re-engage. You can try to outsmart the software by learning the key concepts for which they skim, or you can be proactive and get inside the process:

1. Simplify your résumé. (*This is not the time to be creative.*) Tailor your résumé to match almost word for word the posted job's duties and qualifications. The keywords and terms from the job posting get programmed into the company's tracking software.

2. Find out who the hiring manager is and call him or her. The age-old adage is true, "the squeaky wheel gets the oil." Do not be a nuisance (hence stalker) but always persist. They might agree to see you just to get rid of you. On the other hand, in the age of social media, email, and instant messages, very few people nowadays make phone calls. Pick up the phone, type in those digits, and let it ring. It might be your lucky day!

3. Most larger companies have military recruitment centers. Call and ask to speak with the person in charge of onboarding veterans. Let them know you proudly served your country. Ask if someone might review your

résumé for said position. Next, ask for an interview. Tell them how your experiences align with company goals. Remember, the "ask" is your chance to be seen and is your best shot at getting a leg up on the competition. Frankly, many never make it past the picking phase simply because they don't ask.

4. The brunt of the application process is done online via the company's human resources and recruitment portal, yet applicants rarely think of sending an email. Often, the simplest approach is the most effective. Larger organizations sometimes list their mid-to-senior level staff and their positions on the company's websites. Extract a few names and email away. I have had success doing this with a good response rate.

5. Find an insider who might be willing to refer you. The easiest route is through the receptionists. Get in their good graces, and you will have them eating out your hand. Remember, most receptionists can smell a conman coming from miles away. They screen tens, if not hundreds of calls per day. Let your voice smile and be authentic. You will have a good shot at capturing their interest—and imagination—if you are creative in your approach (*now is the time for creativity*). If you get any information what so ever, follow up with a card, donuts, or latte, expressing your appreciation.

6. Many larger companies offer referral bonuses. I know contractors who make thousands of dollars for referring prospective hires who sign on as employees. Find those persons within an organization, and you will probably walk through the door to a well-paid job.

7.   Write an article or blog post. I caution you, however, if you take this route, also take the time to edit and proofread your work. You will appear more professional if you do, and amateurish if you do not. Did you know that many managers are egocentric and love to share their expertise either as an authority or as a person of high importance? Find someone close enough to the process and ask if you can interview them. Asking the right questions will give you a heads-up into the hiring process.

8.   Contact a business attorney and let him know who you are, what you are trying to do, and why you are qualified to do it. Most business lawyers have and know of clients who are expanding or need to and might be willing to speak with you as a favor to their clients. Use your badge of "veteran" to your advantage!

If all else fails, do what the experts do. In the book, *The Powell Principles: 24 Lessons from Colin Powell, a battle proven leader*, author Oren Harari encourages readers to "let the situation dictate strategy." He writes, "Powell says, 'when the environment changes, you [must] change with it and try to get ahead of it.'"[xv]

Though Powell retired from the military as a hero in the eyes of many, perhaps his greatest legacy will be one of leadership. During times of war, peers and subordinates alike appreciated his trustworthy command. His strategies, while mission-centric, were people-based. General Powell knows that "excellence is a prevailing attitude" and "trust is the essence of leadership."

My environment evolved from one of security to one of the unknown, and, like General Powell, I kept a prevailing attitude. I became single-minded, devised a mission-critical task force, and stopped depending solely on computer-based job searches. Instead, I contacted flesh-and-blood people. In other words, I got out, showed up, and networked.

You see, a computer cannot be programmed to look beneath the human surface. Your very presence has the power to relate, to empathize, to distinguish one emotion from another.

Sometimes, you may not fit the mold of what an organization has programmed themselves to believe about their ideal candidate. That does not mean you give up on your mission. You remain persistent and find other ways to check actions items off your list and show them who you are!

Never doubt your ability to contribute positively to an organization simply because you were not considered for a position. All the same, your training and experiences might land you the interview but it will be your attitude and cooperative spirit that will land you the job.

The Steward Checklist

✓ Finish any school requirements.
✓ Obtain professional certifications.
✓ Make certain to get adequate on the job training (OJT) while still on active duty.

✓ Go for that last promotion. It will be invaluable in establishing your asking price in your civilian job.

✓ If needed, enlist the support of your superiors and peers.

Then:

✓ Contact Human Resource Departments in person and ask if anyone is free to meet with you.

✓ Hand deliver your résumé and get to know the receptionists.

✓ Contact people who work in the company and informally interview them or invite them out for a drink.

✓ Network with folks who know about the organization and get a sense of the company culture.

✓ Find out if they conduct headcount reductions when finding themselves in a financial crunch.

✓ Concentrate on those companies and organizations that are pro-military. This one task will benefit you most in your job search.

✓ Look for friends or separated military inside the organization and glean whatever you can to aid you in your communication with decision makers.

✓ Attend job fairs. As in Walter's case, you never know what impression you will make on a decision-maker. It may result in an interview or job offer.

Please know, I am not talking about Black Ops research and recognizance here; I am merely suggesting you use every means necessary to gain a competitive edge over others in your job search. This exploration requires painstaking diligence and a willingness to think outside of the box.

Hands-down, your military experience gives you a huge advantage if you can connect your skills in ways a lay audience can both understand and appreciate. The former military member's ability to both translate and explain skills gained will be of utmost importance in the quest for gainful employment.

Then and only then will you know what you want to be when you grow up. Take that as a direct challenge to know what makes you tick. American author E.E. Cummings wrote, "It takes courage to grow up and become who you really are."

Subsequently, I performed those exact action steps, and I figured out what I wanted to do when I transitioned out of the military. Fortunately, I had already known what I was good at and what career path I wanted to follow. Years before my retirement I made sure I finished checking all the boxes. Because I had been going to school for a few years before my transition, I found the process to be a fulfilling sojourn. Still, I had to be certain my approach was viable. I did so by:

Fine-Tuning and Executing

One of the hot topics in contemporary business management is strategy execution. I briefly touched on this in the introduction, but it is important you evaluate your progress as you implement your plan. Create realistic, measurable benchmarks that gauge the effectiveness or inefficiency of your plan's various components. What gets measured and rewarded often gets done.

In my timeline example in the pages ahead, you will notice I treated myself to things as I attained certain goals. Purchasing a few items kept me motivated to check off other tasks on my list. Incentives frequently motivate behaviors and often affect positive outcomes. I share with you a story that drives home this point:

> As part of a strenuous training regimen, a group of US Navy Seals were split into smaller teams, with each given the same set of instructions and equipment. Both crews had to perform tasks that would push them to their mental and physical limits. The team outperforming all other crews got a reward of a short respite from additional activities.

> There was a certain "alpha" crew who consistently eclipsed all the teams; hence, they were rewarded most. The head of the cadre decided to perform an experiment and switched the leader of the "alpha" crew with the leader of the "bravo" crew that had the lowest performance.

> One exercise after another showed the bravo crew now outperforming all the other teams, while the performance of the alpha crew invariably reduced to average.

Did this performance enhancement happen because of a change in leadership? Perhaps. As the leader's strategy was studied, it was discovered that he set small goals for his team and rewarded them when they met their target. At other times, the leader would not push his crew as hard, allowing for more autonomy. At the beginning of each exercise, he would communicate his vision to the crew, identify areas of improvement, align his vision with the mission, and measure and reward progress.

Do you know leaders in your organization who have never acknowledged or rewarded the accomplishments of their employees? Similarly, there are managers who over-celebrate, minimizing the efforts of those doing more than is expected of them.

Your job search and future employment depends on successfully finding a balance between risk and reward as you implement these twelve tactics:

1. Identify areas of interest or your personal passion.

2. Evaluate jobs and careers that reflect those interests and passions.

3. Do specific research to determine whether you could see or not see yourself doing the jobs you've identified. (Be honest with yourself.)

4. Apply the Pareto principle to your area of interest (80/20 Rule).

5. Narrow down your job focus to a few industries for which you are willing to work.

6. Further, narrow it down to the 20% of industries holding your interest and playing to your passion.

7. Next, choose the *exact industry* of which you would like to be employed.

8. Then, select the *exact position* within the sector in which you would like to work.

9. Ensure the pay range for this employment opportunity will be enough to sustain the lifestyle you envision for your post-military life. NOTE: A potential employer is not interested in your way of life. Their only concern is what you can do for them. Keep your lifestyle requirements in the forefront of your mind but out of the discussion!

10. Seek out and talk to people in the very field you are interested in working. These individuals will do the legwork for you and you, in turn, will develop a sincere appreciation for them.

11. Be strategic in your pursuit of getting a feel for and understanding what it will take for you to make your professional journey a reality.

12. Once you are confident about the path you want to take, do not hesitate; decide and act.

These foolproof tactics to land a job when transitioning from the military will work for you only with implementation. So often we read, hear, or learn about something that could benefit our lives, but we fail to put it into practice.

Reasons we fail to act vary: lack of motivation and drive, low self-esteem, laziness, cynicism, procrastination. But, quite possibly the root cause of all failures is fear. Much has been explored regarding the fear of failure and its prevalent effect to paralyze individuals to inaction. Still, there are other fears that keep us trapped in a closed mindset, imprisoning us with an unwillingness to branch out to learn anything new that could expand our mind.

In his classic book, *Think and Grow Rich*,[xvi] author Napoleon Hill suggests how to outwit the "six ghosts of fear." He lists these basic fears as:

- The fear of poverty
- The fear of criticism
- The fear of ill health
- The fear of loss of love
- The fear of old age
- The fear of death

As it applies to transitioning and your future career, I place the fear of criticism at the top of the list. You might as well know, your military life and way of doing things will be scrutinized, challenged, and even dismissed in the civilian world. You must develop a tough shell: this is no time to rest on your laurels. I painstakingly reworked what I thought was a doable strategy until I was confident I could have a successful transition. It was a renewed sense of self-confidence that kept the naysayers at bay. Ultimately, everything I present to you is tried and true. You need only follow suit.

Does this mean you must shadow my approach to the letter? No, but I do encourage you to stick to the plan and not waste a lot of time reinventing the wheel for no reason. Why would you? If you only incorporate into your job search those action items that maximize your strengths and minimize your weaknesses, you will see positive results. When you factor in your diverse array of skills, mental fortitude, and persistence, a rewarding career is yours for the taking.

I am aware most military professionals find themselves—perhaps even after they transition—still living the principles in which the various branches of the military inspired in us. Believe me, I know it is sometimes hard to accept that there is life after the military. Core values provide common ground for all individuals in each of the Services.

> Let your actions reflect self-service
> by putting more of yourself before others
> while planning your exit-strategy.

However, people also bring personal convictions to an organization. The interaction between the common ground and the diversity of individual characteristics determine how an organization will function.[xvii] The previous sentence is important to note. Interactions found in the fertile, middle ground of employee relations govern the success or failure of an organization. It is critical for civilian employers to look at individuals who fit the company culture but who can also contribute in unique ways to enhance the whole.

I propose you modify your values and beliefs just a little while executing your transition. Regardless of which branch of the military you belonged, "Honor, Respect, and Commitment" hold true for us all. Keep integrity first for it is by far the most important for any leader.

Remain steadfast to "Loyalty, Honor, and Excellence in all we do" but, as you separate, instead of *Selfless Service* and *Service Before Self*, I suggest you let your actions reflect *self-service* by putting more of yourself before others while planning your exit. It is not selfish; it is wise. Motivational speaker and best-selling author Steve Maraboli writes "How you treat yourself sets the standard for how others will treat you." Set the bar high and demand your worth.

I found it tremendously valuable to visualize my tactics by acting on whatever steps it took to move one step closer to accomplishing my goals. American scholar and leadership expert Warren Bennis reminds us: "Leadership is the capacity to translate vision into reality." No longer bound to an unrealistic ideal, I was freed to prepare for my future. As clichés go, if you fail to plan, you plan to fail. A strategy without execution is merely words on paper never to get checked off.

Proudly, this blueprint is exactly what I used to transition from the United States Air Force successfully. No program, person, or organization offers anything similar. This methodology worked for me, and I know it will work for you. Dwight D. Eisenhower wrote, "In preparing for battle I have always found that plans are useless, but planning is indispensable." Your survival in the civilian workforce depends on careful planning and considering the insights and victories of those who came before you.

The Hustle is Real

The old "hurry up and wait" mentality is a common mindset for some military personnel. This approach never served me well. I am the type who likes to set the wheels in motion. So, once I devised my mental transition, I conducted the research and put in the work to make the physical transition happen.

You might find it difficult to remain focused while following through on plans. I dare not suggest you choose between mission requirements (deployments, long hours) and what your future could be. Each of us must make a choice about what is best for ourselves, our families, *and* the mission. Most of the time these choices are not easy to make, but crucial they are. What is more important; solidifying your post-military career and setting yourself up for success, or winning that service award for NCO or Officer of the quarter? I think you can guess what my choice was.

I advise you to use whatever time you can spare to do whatever it takes to secure your future. Following the principles in this chapter alone will assist you in your quest to transition with confidence and with an awakened desire to serve. It is here for you in black and white. You must only follow the lead.

The hustle comes into play when you devise, follow through, and follow up a regimented course of action you put together on your own. If you are proactive in your search, my methodology will not only help, it will prove its worth with job offers. If you expect the TAP to assure your success, well, I urge you to think again.

Following the roadmap I have laid out, with successful execution you will find yourself smack dab in the middle of the civilian job market, considering a job offer for which you had long planned. Do not wait, do it now, and do it with gusto! General Patton wrote, "A good plan violently executed now is better than a perfect plan executed next week."

Whiskey Tango Foxtrot, over

There was a point when I found things not working to plan, so I called several personal Fragmentary Orders (FRAGO) a few times during my job search. A FRAGO is used to send changes of existing orders to subordinate and supporting commanders while providing notification to higher and adjacent commands.[xviii] I reworked the premise of my orders (my transition plan) until I arrived at a new strategy.

Until I adapted, I struggled. I found the civilian job market perplexing and lacking the structure I had grown accustomed to in the military. The ambiguity of it all was unbearable at times. The hustle came about when I found that my job search plans, as executed, was not working as I thought it should. As a result, the adapt and overcome mentality instinctively kicked in.

Just like Air Force Instruction or General Orders, I realized my plans could have been designed merely to point me in the right direction. What you believe to be the right way is not always the only way. Winston Churchill said, "However beautiful the strategy, you should occasionally look at the results." When those un-foreseen circumstances arise, plan to pivot. You must maintain one foot on the ground while maneuvering the other one in a slightly different direction. Adapt and overcome.

At times, I questioned my planning and execution, but I remained confident in my decision-making abili-ties. Once I decided, I did not second-guess. If some-thing did not work for me, I adjusted accordingly; but, the mission was left uncompromised.

I laid out my personal manifesto in a way that al-lowed for flexibility. I gave myself a few general direc-tives (vectors) and I synchronized them to a timeline. Successful planning requires management of your time if you are to realize your goals by the desired date.

Timeline

• I backward planned my activities from T-12 months, nine months, six months, three months, two months, one month. During each of these phases, I confirmed mission-critical objectives. These vector checks were what led me to ensure I achieved short-term goals. I could then accomplish my bigger goal of a successful military transition.

• I celebrated milestones as I attained goals. Major pur-chases included a few suits to wear during interviews *(answering questions during an interview)*, and having several different résumés written for various positions sought.

- I acquired new skills, followed up on job opportunities, and networked with purpose.
- At quarterly intervals, I reevaluated the effectiveness of each step and adjusted where needed.

Was every highlight monumental? No, they did not have to be. But with each minor victory, I could see my major victory was right around the corner. The age-old proverb "Rome was not built in a day" applies to any plan worth executing. In the article, *Habits, Motivation* by James Clear, he writes "Rome is just the result, the bricks are the system. The system is greater than the goal. Focusing on your habits is more important than worrying about your outcomes."[xix]

Putting it all Together

I often found myself in meetings with people who acted as if they had never heard of the United States military let alone understand its vernacular. I soon realized why some interviewers were confused when I attempted to explain things I believed were easy to comprehend. At first, I thought the interviewers were not even trying to understand what my military experience would bring to their organization.

Luckily, I ran into a person who was prior military, and he explained the dos and don'ts of interviewing. In-a-nutshell, he told me to drop familiar military phrases like Non-Commissioned Officer in Charge (NCOIC), Second in Charge (2IC), and Commander. He advised me to replace those phrases with manager, assistant manager, and Chief executive officer (CEO).

To some, this change in vernacular may be an easy decision, but for me, stuck in the military paradigm for so long, I did not know anything else. After all, I joined the military at 18 years old and retired at 39; it was what I knew.

I have had many conversations with associates who say military people "need" to quickly transition and get a feel for the way the private sector thinks, speaks, and works. These discussions typically begin by stating the lack of experience and accountability leaders have within their respective organizations. In his celebrated book, *Cadence of Care: Imagining a Transformed Advisor-client Experience,* author Tim Owings writes, "The verbs *need, ought,* and *should* cry out for review."[xx] Former colleagues have said to me many times, to have a successful transition from the military to the private sector I *"should"* learn how to maintain my standards and lower the expectations of which I closely held. Dr. Owings may be right!

Every so often I struggle with standards and expectations. I do not believe I must lower my standards but, I am figuring out how to lower my expectations in different situations. A 2014 study published in the Proceedings of the National Academy of Science[xxi] showed people with lower expectations were happier than those with high hopes. The researchers concluded it did not matter as much whether things were going well; what mattered most was if things were going better than expected.

It makes sense; having a higher expectation of an outcome can and will result in disappointment if those expectations are not met or exceeded. Do I believe this? Let us just say I am still working on this one!

So, how does this high/low approach correlate to people in management and leadership positions? And how does a lowered expectation by one affect others? If the group is affected, how does leadership respond? Vince Lombardi appropriately wrote, "The strength of the group is the strength of the leaders." Organizations realizing this truth produce qualified teams able to follow any directive. What is more, employees feel empowered and eager to perform at a higher level.

For me, it was difficult adapting to an environment with team members who may have never bonded together by one general directive that influenced their collective behaviors. Many civilian managers believe military rank and file do not have the aptitude to make a significant organizational difference. They think marketing skills gained in the military do not relate to civilian job requirements. Thus, they fail to see our unique skills as a help rather than a hindrance.

Dealing with people who "think" rather than "know" is one of many issues I faced in my transition. Do not misunderstand; I value thoughtful deliberation and its importance for arriving at conclusions. But, it is crucial for leadership to know certain things, or at the least, know where and how to find the answers.

In ways, I still face obstacles, and yes, at times it is deflating. When this happens, and to remain a team player, I must modify how and what I expect from my civilian colleagues. Unlike lowering my expectations, which is personal, I am now a part of organizational groupthink, which is mutual.

I felt as if I was infiltrating a secret club. In a sense, I was. Only I was the nonconformist who talked softly and carried the big stick. I wanted an opportunity to show everyone I knew my stuff, but I had to respect the boundaries already established and follow the rules. I was, in fact, the FNG on the block. I had no right to shove my leadership acumen in their faces any more than they had the right to blanket me in mindless redundancies. So, I reverted to my strategy to maintain focus. I had to realign with my purpose.

Private organizations are frequently in dire need of capable individuals who can express military tactics to assist in making organizational strategies become a reality. Decision makers, logical thinkers, and empaths have a way of motivating others to achieve company objectives. These individuals are priceless in the private sector. Reminding myself I possesed those attributes, and that I did not need anyone's permission to be self-led, I began leading.

A leader cannot afford to let his or her behavior be lower than the expectations of the team. I know vulnerability is a catch-phrase nowadays, but should a leader convey emotions like fear, despondency, uncertainty, shame? Do you think a show of emotion is an asset or liability?

We all know disappointment abounds when expectations are unmet. What many do not realize, however, is while the admonishment of lower ranks occurs, leadership has already taken the hit. A leader must rise to a self-prescribed level of expectation and remain detached from external influences, including those of his team. Although he must sense and understand the needs of his team members, he must never let his subordinates see him sweat!

You might remember the wrongful death case of Anna Nicole Smith. The presiding judge nearly had an emotional meltdown on national television. He demonstrated such a lack of composure he lost all credibility and was subsequently taken off the case, replaced by another judge.

So, when we lower the bar, how do we reestablish a show of leadership? I reevaluated my next course of action and considered effective leadership as having:

1. a clear vision
2. effective communication
3. operative knowledge within my locus of control
4. the ability to delegate tasks without micromanaging
5. ethical behavior in and out of the office
6. confidence
7. empathy
8. composure in all settings

Stacey Blackman, author of The MBA Application Roadmap: The Essential Guide to Getting *into* a Top Business School, believes Military applicants excel over other candidates because they have dealt with highly stressful situations. She writes, "they think on their feet, make ethical decisions, and lead projects." She continues, "Veterans automatically know how to work in a team and how to earn respect, which is an important characteristic for business school students. M.B.A. programs value this type of experiential knowledge because it gives the applicants a unique perspective during classroom discussions that others are lacking."[xxii]

The personal characteristics top business schools look for in a person are the same qualities that attract human resource executives, headhunters, and employment agencies. If someone possessing the very attributes top business schools look for and a college graduate with no work or life experience was sitting at opposite ends of the table, who would you choose for the job?

☆☆☆☆☆

The Takeaway

There is a significant distinction between changing one's mind and pivoting in a different direction. There will be times after your vector of success has been established when you may be forced to re-examine the underlying assumptions you have embraced throughout your military career into your civilian career.

Prepare for the nuances of your new life as you transition from one sector to the next. Always remember you already have everything it takes to succeed. You need only rely on those commendable traits most servicemen and women acquire over the course of their military careers. When your plan falls short, regroup, rethink, and proceed with confidence.

CHAPTER THREE

TRUST BUT VERIFY:
NAVIGATING THE VA SYSTEM

"A thinker
sees his own actions
as experiments and questions—as
attempts to find out something. Success
and failure are for him answers above all."
Friedrich Nietzsche

Navigating the Veteran Administration (VA) system can be very challenging. I found this lengthy process to be painful as I tried to do it by myself. Discussions with other separated service members concluded the VA might be one of the most underutilized components of the transitioning process.

My experience from both a financial and post-military services perspective proved it could be one of the most rewarding tasks a military professional can do when transitioning to the private sector. Employees at the VA are quite helpful when arming yourself with the knowledge of how to get things done within their parameters. But how do you learn their guidelines?

As with numerous things under the transitioning maelstrom, you must be ruthless in your thirst for knowledge and understanding. Woodrow Wilson stated, "I not only use all the brains that I have but all I can borrow." You too must chisel out every piece of information from every source available if you are to meet your objective of succeeding in a post-military world. Go to every VA sanctioned website and get educated on what and how to correctly gather and post your VA disability claim.

Be fearless asking questions and pushing to find out complete answers to satisfy your curiosity. Instead of stopping with the very first answer you get, continue to probe.

I believe the failure of the masses lies in asking too few questions. It is like buying a used car. You are not going to drive it off the lot without having a thorough

check of the computer, electrical, mechanical, and physical aspects of its operating system. You will inspect the
tires for wear and the body for scratches and dents. You
will take your potentially new vehicle for a test drive. It
does not matter what the salesman says, you will question everything he tells you *and* give the car a complete
once over.

Like the car salesman and other professionals, VA
personnel do not always know the ever-changing rules
and flaws in their systems. However, unlike many other
service related industries, the VA staff's lack of information can and will influence both the money, benefits
and services you have earned and are entitled to receive.

Before I continue to discuss my recommendations
for dealing with the VA, I feel compelled to touch on the
vague sense of ownership most military personnel have
as it relates to the documentation of medical records
during their military career. I know this is a touchy subject for many, but again, I not only speak for myself, but
others as it relates to how we each felt (and continue to
feel) when keeping appointments and seeing the doctor.

Right before military people separate, they can opt
to meet with a VA advocate for guidance filing for disability claims pertinent to their time in the US Armed
Forces. Patient Advocates are highly trained professionals who can help resolve concerns about most aspects of
health care. Most are known to be helpful with those
medical concerns that may have gone unaddressed during the military member's tenure. Many VA advocates
will help get copies of medical records from former
medical treatment facilities the military member had

visited, and will also assist in the filling out of the tedious medical claim forms.

It is not a secret some military supervisors tell their subordinates not to go to the hospital even when the individual probably should go. This type of judgment call oversteps authority and is one of the very reasons many of our folks separate from the military with undiagnosed, untreated, and preventable illnesses. If afforded the necessary medical care available to them at the time, many veterans would not languish in the system. Indeed, subordinates must be trained to be better informed and more outspoken when it comes to rights affecting their personal medical care.

Equally difficult for me to understand were healthcare documentation implications existing within the ranks of the military. When I was active duty, I held two primary positions: Security Policeman for ten years and Aerospace and Operational Physiology technician for eleven.

During my stint in these vastly disparate fields, I was aware of the veiled organizational pressure that led people to shy away from the importance of both treatment and documentation of medical issues. As the saying goes, if undocumented, it never happened! You read it in Michelle's account, and you have probably heard it before, but document, document, document. It will be worth the effort when it is time for you to separate.

One of the things I highly recommend is to find and to stick with, if possible, one good VA representative throughout the numerous phases of your military transition. Even though my advocate did not withhold any information, potentially important steps in the claim process seemed to be unknown. There is a vast amount of information you must understand to success-fully circumnavigate the VA's system: health, education, eligibility requirements, disability benefits, GI Bill, re-tirement, processing, and more.

I had to depend on my research and connections with former military heroes to assist me in getting through the system unscathed. Each one, teach one is a big part of military culture. Use it to your advantage. There are many people genuinely interested in helping you. Seek those members out; they have an abundance of information and experience stored in their knowledge bank.

On the health front, do what you can within your rights to ask for duplicates of your medical records, es-pecially before you transfer to a different base. As a worthwhile practice, I strongly suggest you maintain a personal file of your medical records.

In my case, I had many service related injuries which were dependent on medical and administrative personnel, but I also had copies of my records which proved useful. Because I am a 100% disabled veteran with PTSD, I have an extensive medical file, so I was purposeful in documenting my visits.

I have known too many individuals who reported "lost" medical records when attempting to get proof of injury or illness needed to file a claim. The military healthcare system is just like any other system; shit happens, and records get misplaced. I caution you not to let this unfortunate event happen to you without having a backup of your files.

There are plentiful examples of unfavorable experiences servicemen and women go through when dealing with Veterans Affairs. Volumes of books, websites, news articles, and videos share information on the underpinnings of the VA. You will perhaps find an equal amount of good and bad, guts and glory.

You might recall the recent scandal in which veterans accused the VA agencies of long intervals between appointments, often going months before receiving critical care. Deaths were allegedly occurring because of the lengthy wait times. There were reports of scheduling errors, lapses in referrals to outpatient, specialty, and mental health care services. If that were not enough, undercover investigations exposed hospital personnel siphoning controlled substances for personal use and street sales.

With all this, in 2014 the VA paid out an unprecedented 100 million dollars in bonuses to senior staff, several of whom were under scrutiny for mismanagement and other offenses per an investigative report on CBS News.[xxiii] Not surprising, there remain a culture of mistrust.

I had the privilege of speaking with Tisha, an 11-year veteran who received a medical retirement as determined by the medical board. Her story, wrought with health claims, is due to incompetent or, perhaps overworked, passionless doctors and administrators.

Tisha is from a military family. Her father, brothers, and uncle were all in the military. She enlisted at age 20, deciding after a year of college that higher education was not the road she wanted to go down. She worked one year before deciding to enlist, choosing the Army because her family said promotions in rank were probably the best in this branch of the armed services.

Fort Jackson, SC. was not the best fit for her (she assumed) since she was born and raised in the DC area. Southern charm was not her forte. In fact, she was impatient with it. Tisha, who had the ingenuity of a street hustler, was a typical Type A personality.

Her first injury occurred before basic training graduation when she broke her wrist during hand to hand combat. She then entered a group Physical Therapy Rehabilitation and Evaluation Platoon (PTRP), a hold-over of sorts for soldiers.

Like Tisha's injury, severe strains and broken bones are cause for medical evaluation. Recruits are sent to a rehabilitation platoon for therapy and limited training if deemed unable to continue because of their injuries. Sometimes they are unable to return to a previous unit because the group might have professionally advanced with their military training or have completed basic training altogether. Instead, they join units in the same phase of instruction as when the injury first occurred.[xxiv]

Tisha's hand was not 100% functional, continuing with physical therapy so she could complete the rifle exercises required of all soldiers before completing basic training. With a subpar hand, she later graduated as a private (E-1).

Afterwards, she went to Advanced Individual Training (AIT) for her job as an automated logistical specialist (a beefed-up name for supply technician.) Two years later, after 18 weeks of school, she promoted to the rank of Private Second Class (PV2) and headed to her first real duty station. Placed in a smaller specialized unit, she elevated to E-4, stationed in Hawaii. This duty station was not as glamorous as it might sound.

One day, as Tisha left physical therapy and headed back to work, she was involved in a bad car accident and was transported by ambulance to the hospital. Once there, doctors ran tests and found she had a goiter, though unsure if it was cancerous. Surgeons told Tisha she could die without its removal, offering no second opinion or alternative form of treatment.

First opting not to have an operation, she continued to work. A few months later she elected to have surgery to get rid of the goiter and her thyroid. Unfortunately, the goiter was attached to her vocal chords, so the surgeon removed a part of her vocal chords along with her parathyroid.

After her first thyroid surgery, she was prescribed Synthroid and other drugs. But, instead of regulating her medication, another thyroid surgery was advised. One-and-a-half years later, she gained a lot of weight and began losing her hair. Moreover, she was having stomach and skin issues. Her iron levels were low; she was lethargic and cold all the time.

While still in Hawaii, despite her health issues, she reenlisted so she could use her school option to become a surgical tech. Upon Tisha's transfer to Seattle, she worked in an Ear, Nose, and Throat (ENT) clinic. The doctors, based on her symptoms and repeated sick days, suggested she get a thorough examination. But, before she could schedule one, she was deployed to Iraq. Her dedicated VA specialist fought the deployment to no avail and overseas Tisha went.

About a month before she left Iraq to return stateside, she began having body spasms, cramps, and heart arrhythmias. Doctors again gave Tisha hardly any information about her condition, and she did not press for it either. She was young, away from home, and feeling unwell. But because she did not ask for information, she was given none. Again, we see the usual practice of "don't ask, don't tell." Consequently, Tisha was flown out of Iraq less than a year after arriving due to medical complications.

Tisha was admitted to the hospital over seven times while working in the ENT unit. Each time she was placed on restricted duty, she probably should not have been working at all. Tisha often complained to the doctor that she did not feel right. The Lieutenant Colonel in her command exemplified empathy in leadership. It was he who told Tisha she needed help and should consider the wounded warrior brigade. Subsequently, she enrolled in a few other programs that provided care as well as protect her from being identified as filing false claims.

The False Claims Act is the government's primary civil remedy to redress false claims for government funds, property under government contracts, and programs as varied as Medicare, veteran's benefits, federally insured loans, mortgages, and other assistance programs.

The largest recoveries in recent years involved allegations of fraud and false claims in the pharmaceutical and medical device industries. Of the $2.6 billion in federal health care fraud recoveries, $1.8 billion were from alleged false claims for drugs and medical devices under federally insured health programs, including TRICARE, in addition to Medicare and Medicaid. TRICARE provides benefits for military personnel and their families, veterans' health care programs and the Federal Employees Health Benefits Program.[xxv]

Tisha was unable to get a medical discharge. Her supervisor did everything in her power to get Tisha into a Department of Defense (DoD) sponsored program for 8-16 weeks. She had therapy, one-on-one, and group sessions.

During therapy one day, she revealed for the first time she had seen her best friend die on the job. While stationed in Iraq, her responsibility was to receive both deceased and injured soldiers for processing through the system. She would one day receive her closest friend as a casualty after his unit got ambushed while on a mission. He was one of four American heroes who died that day.

Unaware that she suffered from Post-Traumatic Stress Disorder (PTSD) or any other kind of emotional trauma, Tisha established a new normal. She was a little depressed losing her friend but never considered a psych disorder could be triggering her emotional state

even though she had been on the front line during combat operations. PTSD was one of a multitude of service-
related injuries for which she would eventually receive
treatment and disability classification.

Tisha experienced a lot of undocumented care.
There was nothing in her official medical charts: no
prescriptions, dosages, diagnoses—nothing. So, how
could she prove her claims? When she returned stateside, what little documentation she did have, did not follow her to her next duty station. Each time she went to
a new location, her records were supposed to follow, but
they did not arrive. Her dental records were left unac-
counted. Most of her medical records were incomplete
or "missing." At one point her entire history was lost.

Again, we see a recognizable pattern surfacing. The
ENT doctor for whom Tisha worked advised her, going
forward, to document every sniffle, cough, and specifi-
cally, every doctor's appointment and hospital visit. After that, like clockwork every two to three months Tisha
got printouts of her encounters and kept meticulous records. She had a trail of documentation which proved
useful in her disability claim.

If you take nothing else from her account, let this
serve as a reminder to vigilantly document every encounter, phone call, or actual office visit. If ever you
have doubts as to whether you should submit a
document, do so, but keep the originals. Always send
copies!

Tisha received briefings on The Army Career and
Alumni Program (ACAP), a mandatory program for
transitioning soldiers from active duty. One of the many

services under this program is a pre-separation meeting which includes benefits information and guidance relevant to a successful transition. Through ACAP, pre-separation planning is congressionally mandated by Public Law 107-103.

Separating Soldiers, irrespective of rank, are required to receive counsel and the DD Form 2648 at least 120 days before expiration- term of service (ETS.) Under this service agreement soldiers contractually acknowledge they are free to either leave the military or re-enlist and continue their military service on a specified date.

It is important to mention, as part of a recently improved ACAP system, soldiers can now begin transitioning 12 to 18 months before separating.[xxvi] I again encourage you to start the process early. Doing so, the more successful you will be in seamlessly transitioning from enlisted to civilian-employed.

When Tisha enrolled in a pilot program overseen by a medical board, she saw a slew of doctors who evaluated how sick she was and if she was, in fact, unfit for duty. She was eventually deemed 90% unfit for duty by the army and 100% by the VA.

An advocate began working with Tisha to help her keep appointments, bringing us to another important point: when you collaborate with a Veteran's Service Organization (VSO), advocates can take you further than you might get on your own. These associations know how to deal with the VA and can ensure your paperwork is complete and correct.

Nevertheless, this does not mean you should stop advocating for yourself. And please remember, be wary of any organization or support who charges you for help with your VA claim. They may be trying to take advantage of your unfortunate situation.

The transition process for Tisha was a double-edged sword. On the one hand, it was frustrating because there were so many unknowns. On the contrary, it was enlightening because she learned things she would not have, had she transitioned on her own (which many service men and women inevitably are forced to do). Tisha was one of the fortunate few who would have never known what she now knows had it not been for the pilot program in which she participated.

After months of red tape, Tisha realized:

- She was eligible for social security immediately after her diagnosis of "unfit for duty." (Eventually, with the assistance of a disability attorney, she received a substantial sum from a back-pay settlement)
- There were numerous out-patient programs available to her.
- There was an assortment of In-patient programs in which she could have joined.
- She could participate in family, individual and group therapy until accepted into the pilot program.
- She could have received alternative therapies like acupuncture and chiropractic medicine early in her illness.

- The wounded warrior brigade exclusively serves wounded soldiers who are either pending medical separation, retired or unfit for duty.
- There was a program called Chapter 31: VA Vocational Rehabilitation Education Program. This education benefit was separate from the GI bill.
- While the TAPs and ACAP initiatives prepare you for life after the military, you must be proactive in your quest for information. Tisha learned how to fill out paperwork. Both programs taught her how to translate many of her military acquired skills to civilian duties.

After Tisha received her medical rating, she was sent to learn a new vocation. She could choose from any number of schools and majors, so she decided to attend The Art Institute of Washington and major in photography.

She is now in the AW2, the official U.S. Army program that assists and advocates for severely wounded, ill, and injured soldiers, veterans, and their families, wherever located, regardless of military status. She is eligible to be followed for five to ten years-post-military.

Tisha's VA advocate emails her every two or three months to check on her health, to offer job search assistance, or simply to talk. She has follow-up appointments at the VA a few times per month and takes advantage of that frequency because her visits keep her actively in the system. When regularly seen, you do not go through the same redetermination rigors as one with less visits.

I caution you, as does Tisha, to retain copies of every record, including prescriptions, office visits, consults, sick days—everything! If the VA needs more medical information to verify your claim, they may ask you to provide it.

You will probably undergo a medical evaluation to assess the disabilities for which you are eligible. If you are required to have an examination that could support your assertions, make it a point to show up on time for the appointment or risk having your claim delayed or denied.

The VA might schedule you for multiple medical appointments depending on how many or what type of disabilities you claim. Even if you think you are feeling better, go! Do not chance a lapse or discontinuation of benefits unless you have improved health sustained for consecutive years. Old injuries often come back to haunt you, as you will soon read in Paul's case. Your benefits will stay the same only if your condition remains the same or gets worse. Disappointingly, many individuals are bent on defrauding the system, which is one reason the application and approval process is so daunting.

If you are not privy to the information out there, you are out of luck. Tisha receives Army medical retirement, social security disability, education assistance, alternative therapies, and she is still entitled to her GI Bill benefits. She used active duty funds for her first degree. Her second degree was through the Department of Veteran Affairs (DVA). Had she not been in the medical field, working under concerned, helpful managers, she might not have known her entitlements.

Tisha, at long last, received her medical discharge in 2013, although her separation date was 2011. For two years, considered active duty, she continued to receive her paycheck. She again stresses, "Claim everything and document even when you do not make claims." Upon separation from any of the armed services, you must be able to prove an injury is "service connected" [xxvii] or your application will more than likely get stamped "denied."

You served your country; now, you must take care of yourself by utilizing the massive pool of resources available to you. Understanding the various steps in the process is the first line of business. Tisha learned, perhaps the hard way, the ins-and-outs of the system without egregiously taking advantage of it. She appreciates the dedication of her advocate and values the solidarity among members of the wounded warrior program.

There is a similar camaraderie and shared loyalty in many of the programs you will discover in your ongoing pursuit of support channels. Take advantage of every morsel of information, every program, every advocate. Many of your predecessors could not as the following story illustrates.

Paul B. joined the Navy as part of a voluntary draft after flunking out of college one year into a football scholarship. He signed on for a four-year stint. A battery of tests determined what discipline he would be best at and he began life in the military as a dental prosthetics technician. He shared with me his stories of life during the Vietnam War.

Medical concerns, he says, were not addressed, even if you were severely sick. There were many unreported illnesses during the Vietnam War era. Agent Orange was routinely dumped and sprayed indiscriminately from airplanes onto fields, jungles, and soldiers who did not dare take off their boots when walking through the thick brush and parasite infested mud. If doing so, their feet would get wet with corrosive chemicals, and the skin would swell and peel. Paul described the toxic exposure to his skin as a burning sensation from the inside out. He recalls a time when he took off his boots and rodents ate the dead, flaky skin of his feet. His extremities were so numb he could not feel the rats gnawing at his skin or the insects attacking his flesh.

Once exposed, the men were told to take showers because, at the time, human response to chemical exposure and its effects were unknown. Soldiers, pumped with tetanus shots, continued to perform their duties under the worse of circumstances and conditions.

Like Paul and Walter, a lot of men who served in Vietnam went without diagnoses. Many had symptoms indicating something was wrong, but they did not go to the VA for a multitude of reasons. Some were psychologically broken and did not have the support system needed to address medical concerns. It was overwhelming. Paul knows of several men who committed suicide due to the lack of adequate mental health care. Others went about life with a sense of bravado, refusing to allow the ravages of war to assault their bodies.

Some thought, and still think there is considerable red tape attached to the VA. They do not want to go through the litany of paperwork and necessary follow-up for additional services.

Still others, like Paul, were climbing the corporate ladder pursuing the promise of the American dream.

Paul traveled worldwide as an executive on a transportation research board with the Clinton Administration. The lure of money and success kept him preoccupied and busy. He did not have the time or the inclination to stop and think about his health. Unfortunately, illness found Paul. He developed a host of infirmities, most notably PTSD and prostate cancer.

It took him a while to get sufficiently diagnosed and to secure benefits to which he was entitled, but he persisted. Today, Paul receives the care he needs and gets adequate treatment for his illnesses. He collects full disability under a compensation provision for veterans exposed to Agent Orange or other herbicides during military service. Two of his illnesses, diabetes and prostate cancer fall under the "presumptive diseases"[xxviii] which are associated with Agent Orange exposure.

Paul thinks the VA lacks the qualified personnel to offer the scope of care most veterans require and deserve. He is not saying that some VA employees are not doing a good job but, he encourages you to become your own advocate. "Your participation in the claims process must be proactive," advises Paul. "And, documentation is critical. Without it, you end up in a gray zone when you cannot provide the necessary papers to support your claim."

He believes once you receive your rating, you are in a safe zone. If you feel you deserve a higher rating, you must have your documentation in order. It could take years of back and forth, filing and re-filing, going before committees, and more. Remember, you are one of the thousands going through the claims process. Do not languish in the system without hope. It is wiser to prepare and stay one step ahead of the pack than to go without care.

James R., another Army friend of mine, found the same to be true. However, he is one of those success stories who had good people in his corner. Without competent leadership, he sees how his situation might be different.

A series of back problems while overseas introduced James to the world of medical claims. At first examination, he was having normal duty-related aches and pains. As the problem persisted, he was diagnosed with a disc injury and subsequently underwent back surgery. He spent three months in rehab.

Like Tisha, he was deployed overseas because warm bodies were needed but, once he had surgery, he was considered medically non-deployable. To keep from getting a declination statement, he volunteered to go abroad. A declination statement in the long term can kill a military career.

Circumstances suggest we are strongly encouraged to volunteer. But, the truth of the matter is you are often in a difficult situation. Does the detail have the facility to meet your medical needs? If surviving for a year, you must find out where you will work as a medically non-deployable because now are labeled as such.

Fortunately, like Tisha, James was placed in a warrior transition unit (WTU). There he was privy to the multitudes of benefits available to him. ACAP is five days. In contrast, the WTU lasts a few months, during which time you are not to work in your regular job. The main objective is to heal and transition.

James was assigned several counselors and services; medical, mental health, career, and legal. While attending his transition program, James discovered his military qualifications did not necessarily translate to a civilian position. Because he prepared in advance and had the right support, his passage from enlisted to civilian was smooth. He says he got lucky. But Tony Robbins says, "The meeting of preparation with opportunity generates the offspring we call luck."

With one year of transition preparation, James was allowed the opportunity to put everything in place. His transition team gave him time to meet the right people who pointed him in the right direction. He considers it a fluke that he got hooked up with a golf program. I say it was because he researched, followed up with ideas, and was not afraid to try something new.

He saw an ad for the Golf Academy of America and went to speak with a PGA professional at a local golf course. One thing led to another and, with the support and guidance of leadership, James is now studying golf management at the Academy under a disability vocational rehab program.

You too can use the vocational rehab bill in conjunction with your GI bill. Different career paths determine the various use of the bill. Using a post 911 GI bill in a nine-month block benefits him in this situation. Find counselors who can help you put together specific educational packages that best fit your unique situation.

Seek out those professionals and be a sponge: soak up every piece of knowledge you can.

As in any arena, the better prepared you are the more likely you are to succeed. You have access to a multitude of services and information. Do not stop until you have received all of which you are entitled. Even when you are unsure, ask. As I have mentioned earlier, in almost every area in life, if you fail to ask, you might never know. But, once you know, act.

☆☆☆☆☆

The Takeaway

In any arena, you must compete for what you want and deserve. Without a fight, there is no victory. Devise a doable strategy to navigate the intricacies of the VA system. Think creatively. Be receptive to those willing to help you along the way. You will encounter many who have lost their passion for service, although there are just as many who are prepared to lend a helping (and knowledgeable) hand. But, relying solely on your advocate keeps you out of the loop and uninformed. Treat your health advocacy like a call to arms and position yourself to win. Most of all, document, document, document.

CHAPTER FOUR

EMBRACE THE SUCK

History
has demonstrated that
the most notable winners usually
encountered heartbreaking obstacles
before they triumphed. They won because
they refused to become discouraged by their defeats.
B.C. Forbes

Those who have never served have difficulty understanding the phrase "Embrace the suck!" or "Suck it up Buttercup!" What this means is a person must come to grips with him or herself and know that while the present situation may be bad, they accept the fact the situation sucks, but they must perform at their highest level anyway.

Once you acknowledge yes, this is a SNAFU (the situation is f*cked up), but it is a normal state of affairs, i.e., war stinks, innocent lives are lost, family and friends disappear, you either plunge into despair, or you rise to the occasion. I hope you do the latter.

It is hard to stay depressed too long when you have shared life-changing experiences with members of your unit. You form a brotherhood/sisterhood. It is hard to explain how and why that bond forms, but your comrades in times of war become your family under the stars and stripes.

As Paul B. says, "You cannot go to war without forming bonds with the men and women you fight beside. You cannot join the military and come out non-patriotic. We have a shared and genuine belief that America is the greatest country in the world."

I treasure the lifelong friendships I have with those whom I have proudly served our country. I confidently speak for many others who share the same sentiment.

My good friend "Dozzi" (yes, most military people pick up a nickname of sorts, given to them because they did something funny or stupid, or as a shortened version of their name) was a frontline supervisor when we first met. Here we were, an E-4 and an E-2, bonding as equals. He told me things like: "Make sure you go to school. Make sure you volunteer for things. Make sure you study so you can get promoted."

Most of his words were good advice, but because I was a thick-skulled, cocky 19-year-old, first time away from home, good looking young man—yes, I said it— with a certain curiosity for the ladies, I did not want to hear it! I wanted to work hard and play even harder.

Even though there were times when I did not want to hear him out, to this day, I thank him. I appreciate Dozzi and people like him who took the time to care about my well-being and future. I needed someone like Dozzi to remind me I was not going to stay young forever and my older, wiser self would one day appreciate the guidance. Man, was he right! His persistent voice in my ear helps keep me grounded even to this day.

Having people who care enough to correct you when you are about to head down the wrong path or to ensure you are staying on the correct one, in my opinion, is in short supply in the private sector. Having respect for people does not mean you agree with everything they do and say, or turn a blind eye when they are doing or saying something wrong. No, respecting others means having the courage to address their attitudes and behaviors when they are underperforming or they are in danger of heading down the wrong path.

It has been my experience that many in the private sector look at their livelihood as a job and not as a career. Consequently, some civilians remain detached and less willing to form relationships outside of occasional small talk in the lunch room.

Also, I find civilians at times have doom and gloom attitudes whereas the former military member, in many cases, is simply happy to be alive providing value to his or her employer and comrades. The military culture also requires you to become "your brother's keeper." It is altogether a different dynamic than what I have thus experienced in the civilian world.

I miss the camaraderie and closeness I experienced with other service men and women. I long for the family-like bond we shared with one another while on and off duty. A lot of the Airmen I worked and served with came from different states, many of different backgrounds and ethnicities. We were always together, like a close-knit family, and we discovered we had many things in common.

Where are the mentorships and the listening ears? What happened to the brotherhood? I long for an environment that understands it is a form of therapy to share frustrations with your co-workers as you try to figure things out. I want the non-judgmental community where it is okay to admit I do not know everything. In the face of insecurities and a pile of uncertainties, it was always one team, one fight!

Effective leadership places value on the close relationships of his or her subordinates. We have all heard it many times: a team is only as strong as its weakest link. Yes, worlds sometimes collide, and coworkers do not always get along. I understand spirits of jealousy and pettiness are pervasively rooted in fear of the unknown. I also acknowledge I have an obligation, perhaps self-imposed, to uphold the Airmen's Creed despite my occupation or place of employment. "I am an American Airman. Wingman, Leader, Warrior."

Whenever I feel out of sorts, like I am the weakest link, I think of my friend Sean and his wife, Keisha. They both hail from New York City; I, from Houston. Sean and I hung out and played basketball together quite a bit at my first duty station. I remember long, passionate discussions about the best city to be born and raised and who, during our enlistment, were the greatest basketball teams. He sided with the New York Knicks; I naturally sided with the Houston Rockets.

It was always a pleasant diversion to argue over the best of whatever was the topic at hand. It is funny how, when disagreements arise, no matter how innocent, it is easy to have a sense of superiority. You know what you know, right? As contradictory as it sounds, I suppose it is the competitive edge the military stirs in me that allows me to get such a kick out of a raucous, yet silly practice. I want the same sense of familiarity (and workplace diversions) with my coworkers.

I am reminded of a training session about two years' post-military service, during which I crossed paths with a woman, perhaps in her mid to late fifties. We were talking about the difference between two approaches when she asked me if I had ever served in the military. I answered her with a resounding "Yes! Proudly for 21 years."

She answered, almost condescendingly, "Oh, that explains a lot."

"Why would you make such a statement?" I asked. Her comment had peaked my curiosity.

"I've been doing my job for 20 years," she said. "The only ones who ever pushed work back to me were my supervisor and people who had served in the military." She continued, "Military people live and make leadership decisions in combat that affect people's lives, but the work we are doing isn't life and death." Pausing for a moment, she finished her diatribe with, "Our job situations don't require such a detailed way of doing things. People's lives are not on the line here. You really *should* relax and acclimate to how the private sector operates."

Therein lies the military-civilian dichotomy. On the one hand, she is right. We are not making critical decisions per say. Lives are not at stake; but, livelihoods are. Should we not dedicate as much pride in our outcomes as if it were life and death? For many people, their lives *are* dependent on their livelihood. As a side note, I work in a healthcare environment where people's lives are on the line every day.

On yet another side note (which I briefly touched on in a previous chapter), the field I work in promotes the use of Standardized Work which identifies and details best practices, allowing everyone to operate in the same manner. Understanding what can improve, we advance daily operations in a sustainable manner.

Lean, Six Sigma, and Theory of Constraints are extensively recognized problem-solving methodologies that enhance operational efficiencies. With the use of these emerging practices, we find new ways of doing things, and these enhancements become the baseline for future improvements. This method is part of what the civilian sector calls training within industry (TWI). Military or civil servants refer to it as Standard Operating Procedures (SOPs).

The conversation continued as she accused the military of conditioning me in such a way that it was keeping me from accepting my new role as I transitioned from the war encumbrances of the Air Force. You should have seen my face and body language! I, with poise and grace, listened to her rant before I stuck out my chest and proudly stated, "Yes, I am honored to be a former military leader."

In rebuttal, I shared with her my observations while in the air force and how the lack of a clear direction cost the lives of airmen I had the privilege of serving alongside. I discussed my view of a select group of people under the umbrella of the private sector, who had received their leadership positions, in part, because of luck, who they knew, and natural attrition, instead of expertise and an ability to lead.

Case in point: a manager left the company, and an immediate vacancy arose. Obvious choices for a replacement had either retired or moved on to greener pastures. This vacancy left the organization with a perceived gap and a job position to be advertised and filled.

Most mid-level employees had no mentors, nor were they trained to be like the great leaders I had the pleasure of serving under during my military tenure. I explained that from day one in the air force, we are taught to take charge of those around us when the current person in charge is no longer available to perform his or her duties.

The "be all you can be" mentality is unique to the United States Armed Forces. The military encourages its members to take on leadership responsibility and training.

It is my practice as a leader for those under me to be accountable for the development of their "one down," or the next person in the chain of command. Sometimes called 2IC or second in charge, the 2IC is responsible for the development of his or her "one down" and so on. This level of accountability does not end until it reaches the lowest person in the organization.

Taking advantage of this tiered approach, an organization can focus on the continual development of their people to promote from within the ranks. A close advisor to former Secretary of State Colin Powell, American diplomat Richard Haass wrote, "You cannot be effective if those who work for you are not. So, building their effectiveness ought to be a priority." With that in mind, the "one down" method can develop future leaders and become the glue upholding the corporate ethos.

An organization's members, whose collaborative energies shape a company's footprint, often welcome change. In this regard, the "each one, teach one" approach can further those efforts. As such, there are ways leaders can change the organizational footprint in their given industry:

1. Focus on recruiting the right talent that mirrors the organization's culture.

2. Emphasize the professional development of subordinates which enhance the strengths and drive of the individual.

3. Concentrate on promoting from within to retain exceptional talent.

It has been my observation that some individuals come into a corporate environment with the goal of making a name for themselves by highlighting their previous military role. These persons then make promises that things will be different under their watch. Often, no changes occur.

Indeed, there are similar types of people in leadership positions existing in the military as well. One of the major differences between military and civilian methods of training is how an organization welcomes a new leader.

It is not unusual for a newly assigned officer to want to immediately take charge upon his or her arrival; but, in fairness, I have experienced the same in the civilian sector.

In contrast, successful military leaders gather the advice of senior folks who have been there with what we describe as "boots on the ground." This phrase means they are the experts, possessing invaluable knowledge and experience in their area of expertise that you will not find in any SOPs or policy manuals.

These experienced individuals know what is going on and can be of great assistance in explaining the lay of the land to the newly appointed leader (whom I have seen barking out commands only to find out they were incredibly wrong). Most quickly learn that the errors in their decision-making create grave consequences to themselves, their teams, the people around them, and the organization.

My experiences have taught me that most civilian managers fall somewhere in the middle. Many of these individuals—despite good intentions—are ill-equipped to shape the success of a team. Often it is because they fail to accurately size up the individuals on their teams. Everyone has a backstory that affects their attitudes, beliefs, and yes, performance.

That said, I have also seen military leaders who have learned, sometimes the hard way, that it is wise to first assess the culture before attempting to establish his or her dominance. Those same individuals turn out to be effective leaders.

The newly assigned leader may want to huddle up with subordinates and department experts to get a grasp of the conditions existing within the organization and get an accurate feel of what has occurred in the past as well as today's challenges. In *A Legacy of 21st Century Leadership*, authors Jim Trinka and Les Wallace appropriately write, "Feedback is a gift. Ideas are the currency of our next success. Let people see you value both feedback and ideas." [xxix]

What is needed:

1. Gather and understand background information. You cannot lead in the dark unless you are familiar with the terrain.

2. Grasp the current situation without making assumptions. Isaac Asimov said, "Your assumptions are your windows on the world. Scrub them off every occasionally, or the light won't come in."

3. Have a revealing discussion with the senior person in charge who can shed light on the situation.

Behind closed doors and out of public sight, most successful military officers have a heart-to-heart with their senior enlisted person. This a useful exercise, beneficial to whoever takes over a leadership position. During this discussion, it is of utmost importance the senior enlisted leader is a no-nonsense type of person who can tell it as it is for the sake of the organization's forward thrust. If it is not a forthright individual, the conversation is futile.

But, if a leader is already placed, the newly assigned officer can be briefed on current affairs. I encourage the recently designated civilian manager, supervisor, or his or her counterparts, to each adopt and practice this tried-and-true exercise when first placed in a position of unexpected leadership.

As an apt parallel, we often see this heart-to-heart, or an intimate exchange of ideas, shared concerns, and victories, played out over a round of golf. Most who punish themselves with this game of skill and precision know there are management principles at its very foundation.

Similarities between the sport and leadership are endless. The six Ps describe both the aspects of leadership as well as the game of golf.

**Proper Preparation Prevents
Piss Poor Performance**

In golf, if one does not prepare, or practice correctly, the game suffers. I have yelled "fore!" more times than I care to admit after hitting errant balls. I have triple-bogeyed on par fours after I ended up in sand traps and regularly shoot more than I would like. Even still, I have played with worse. It should come as no surprise that those who occupy themselves with the sport regularly, who take lessons, and practice often, realize the best scores.

While playing, if you make a mistake, you cannot blame it on a teammate; it is on you. Likewise, the head of an organization is accountable and held responsible for the outcomes the organization produces. A leader with integrity does not place blame on anything or anyone other than him or herself. He accepts full responsibility for his or her conduct and attitudes.

On the golf course, we uphold the highest level of integrity. Trustworthiness is expected of every man and woman before he or she hits a ball from the first tee. Owing to the solitary nature of the sport, you might find yourself in easily manipulable positions. But, integrity demands "you do what is right even when no one is looking." You suck it up and move to the next hole. Similarly, effective leadership is not easily biased, influenced, or mastered, only improved.

Leadership lessons are central to the game of golf and can be applied by anyone. Through trial and fire, James, who we met earlier, applies those lessons to his daily life and believes he is a better man because of what he has learned on the golf course. He credits his love for the game with his time spent in the army.

James' military career began soon after he completed a year and a half of college as a premedical biology student at Virginia Commonwealth University in Richmond, Virginia. It was a top tier school, but James was not quite ready for prime time. He was not prepared to put in the work. James was a C student in high school, excelling in the subjects he preferred, failing in the ones he did not like.

An only child in a two-parent household, some might consider him lucky. He was never at a loss for parental guidance. Both grandparents were in close contact with him as well. Nevertheless, his mom counted the days he would be out of the house. She made it uncomfortable for him to stay home.

With military roots going back to Tiger Cub Scouts and ROTC, joining the military was the easiest route for James to take. He told his mom college was not working in his favor. Soon afterward, military recruiters came by the house. The Army proved the best sell for him, and he enlisted.

James is one of many veterans who, despite hardships on and off the battlefield, overcame limitations to course a new life for himself.

He separated from the military a few years ago, when his back injury left him unfit for duty. A neurosurgeon once asked him if he played golf or tennis. "If those vertebrae do not get rotational exercise" he cautioned, "your condition will worsen." So, James began lessons. He is currently in school for golf management and is considered a golf professional with a handicap of seven.

In golf, you can hire a coach who will work on the progression of your game by building on your existing foundation—psychological and physical—to help you retain good habits while working on the bad ones. For me, I must keep my head still and focus on the ball during my swing. A golfer who lifts his or her head during the swing to see where the ball is heading, often finds their body unaligned only to hit the ball in an unintended direction.

Recreational golfers, as well as the pros, have the same issues on the golf course. Each must practice and train to establish good form. The same applies to a leader. Just like a golf swing, it is of utmost importance to "maintain balance" in leadership. Moreover, one needs to exercise sound judgment, integrity, and comradery to effectively understand the game's culture.

Coincidentally, part of my professional expertise is the changing of an organization's culture, allowing the leadership team to provide value to their customers by capitalizing on the skill set and mindset of its employees. However, what good is a skill if you do not have the proper tools to produce the desired results?

To change the culture, the leaders of a group can attempt to force their thoughts, feelings, and beliefs on individuals within the organization. Those employees might produce mediocre results at best. But an effective leader will, at a minimum, improve the quality, delivery, and cost (QDC) of your product or service.

Not all employees are focused on the same deliverables, so I coach them to see how aligning what is relevant to internal capabilities links to the overall mission, vision, and values of the Coalition. I help them develop, deliver, and execute their organizational strategy to the point of greatest impact at every level in the organization.

So, how does this relate to the game of golf? Well, I do not know a soul who plays golf who does not want to improve his or her game. If the golfer is not committed to practicing differently those things that will enhance his or her performance, they will have a tough time developing as a good player. The best leaders I have ever come across have been committed to learning from their mistakes and finding new and innovative ways to unlearn ineffective practices.

A leader is charged with and accountable for the professional development of his or her people. That means the leader must develop himself with the attributes of leadership: confidence, decisiveness, passion, focus, to name but a few. These are the very qualities turning a bad golfer into a good one, and a good golfer to a great one.

When you look at yourself with sobering honesty, you begin to see your flaws as well as your strengths. Only then can you empathize enough with others to help them grow personally and professionally.

Like the game of golf, you know perfecting your swing is a journey without a destination. Yes, consider your flaws and strengths without focusing on results. It is all about the incremental improvements you make along the way. And, like any effort, you reap the by-products:

Resilience: That remarkable ability to bounce back after defeat. Legendary golfer Arnold Palmer said, "The most rewarding things you do in life are often the ones that look like they cannot be done." Resilience evokes a spirited determination and keeps you chasing the perfect swing on and off the golf course.

Flexibility and the notion that pivoting is different from changing one's mind or heading in a new direction. When executing a task, if one way does not work, it is wise not to buckle. You must try other ways to accomplish your goal. Social entrepreneur Ryan Lilly wrote, "Change occurs when excuses pivot to execution." When you have the inner vision, foresight, and strength needed to know when and where to bend, you awaken the leader within.

Situational Awareness (SA): what has happened, what is happening, what will happen in the future. Do you remain acutely aware of past and present events and how they directly or indirectly impact your mission? Can you find your ball in the rough?

Intestinal Fortitude: I share with you an old army truism which states, "Coffee tastes better if the latrines are dug downstream from an encampment." Put another way, when the oscillating rotator engages the fecal matter (when the shit hits the fan), where are you standing?

As it stands, many of the qualities I once believed to be the holy grail of growth no longer hold sway with me. Maybe my military career ingrained certain traits in my psyche and have become part of who I am. In any event, you live, you learn, and if lucky, you play golf. You travel from point A to B along life's fairways. You adapt to the changing landscape without it changing you. You outgrow people, places, and things. You evolve and get better.

Still, these very traits remain an extraordinary reach for many of my civilian contemporaries who stay locked in a groupthink mindset. Effective leadership does not rely solely on one type of management style. Nor does it discount the unique skill set of its subordinates. Not everyone is empowered to contribute, to share ideas, to innovate. You must be exemplary on your own, covertly, until someone takes notice.

When I am bogged down with activities I feel are run-of-the-mill, that do not stretch my imagination or allow me to utilize my talents, I get bored but complete the task with a newness of thought. And yet, some of my colleagues often go crazy over what is believed to be the "latest and greatest innovation."

Maybe there is value in holding such an attitude; but, viewpoints vary on the subject. Nevertheless, for me and my military background, it is often a case of been there done that so let us venture on to something truly new and inspiring.

As a civilian, I, perhaps like you, struggle with the non-motivated people with whom I work and their resistance to being held accountable for their part in organizational outcomes. On a weekly basis, I wrestle with adjusting to personalities who lack strong moral character. The blatant lack of respect for authority exists at every level.

I am not referring to the frustrated water cooler small talk among junior staff discussing their superiors; this type of banter exists in both military and civilian populations regardless of position. I refer to the "protect my ass" mentality of those who have a personal agenda and are in it for themselves.

When you find yourself in an environment far removed from the core values you espouse, keep from getting caught in the undertow. Thomas Jefferson reminded us "In matters of style, swim with the current; in matters of principle, stand like a rock." You must never arrive at a place of apathy; it is unfair to your coworkers, organization, and yourself.

One of the distinct differences between military and civilian personnel, to me, is how they respond to stressful situations. I mean not to downplay the many men and women with whom I work who exhibit unmatched levels of excellence; however, that *is* a blanket statement covering a select few.

When I was on active duty, I was accustomed to taking and executing orders to produce the desired result in an organized and timely fashion. As I accelerated in rank and responsibility, the more directional the commands became, and more was expected of me to carry out those directives. Persons above me gave orders that produced a vector, or general direction, and it was up to me to determine how to achieve the objective.

I find it difficult to develop comparable relationships in the civilian world where a team of co-workers share life-altering experiences while executing a mission each deems relevant. I do not think our military brotherhood is better than our civilian counterparts, but I have accepted we have been trained to socialize (and support one another) in a very different way.

I am by no means suggesting ex-military are saints who walk on water. Admittedly, I am somewhat short on patience, especially with mediocrity. I believe a lot of military members take the stance they too are impatient which may cause issues when working in the private sector. When we do or say something second nature to us, we mistakenly are judged as coming off arrogantly.

If a colleague is not going all out or at full throttle in what they do, it is disappointing. Military members, when faced with a directive, are expected to tackle it.

When encountering problems, nine times out of ten he or she will first attempt to overcome the obstacle before looking for direction. We believe when in doubt, work it out! The success or failure of a mission is at stake.

Many military members can tell immediately whether a person will be dedicated and productive or not. Those colleagues who are unmotivated in the small things are the hardest to work with or for; beware! Never look at a company and its employees through rose-colored glasses. There is always a weak link. Make certain it is not you.

There exists a corporate ethos which suggests employees immediately water down anything that might incite confrontation. Effective, mature communication among the adults I have encountered is gravely lacking, perhaps if for no other reason than it is not proactively encouraged.

You may be familiar with those work environments where it is frowned upon to strike up friendly conversation with your cubicle associates outside your assigned lunch hour. Should you venture down such a path, you may get pegged as slacking on the job or not taking your career seriously. This type of work environment is neither healthy nor productive.

Now to briefly side with my civilian counterparts, not all senior enlisted are qualified to be managers in the corporate world. Some are unable to separate far enough from the disciplined military life to adapt to the attitudes and mindsets of their colleagues in a collaborative environment.

I also know many civilian managers must deal with a level of pettiness with some subordinates: the bathroom gossip, the lack of self-initiative—or worse—the whiner who either incessantly complains over whose job it is to do what, or never admits to a wrong. There is also the chronic over-achiever who wants to take credit for anything good but is quick to distance him or herself when something is amiss.

This type of inconsequential BS can be overwhelming at times and does little to further the success of the team. Counterintuitively, however, these behaviors do allow the manager to identify those individuals serving as the ball or the chain.

☆ ☆ ☆ ☆ ☆

Back to the conversation I had with the older woman in my organization: you know, the one who told me I "should" calm down and learn to relate to the private sector way of life. After explaining my expectations to her, I expounded on one of the many reasons military people feel a sense of togetherness. Based on the construct of responsibility existing within the military, managers and their subordinates naturally become closer and more involved with one another.

Before I could continue, this woman, who at first was a little defensive, settled to a place of listening attentively, as if she was trying to understand. Still, she was harboring something that did not reckon with the preconceived ideas to which she so tightly held. Then, mid-sentence and without warning, she interrupted me (as if she had a lot of feelings on her mind or heart) to share a very personal story of her own.

She told me: "My son had been in the US Marine Corps. Eight weeks in, he was diagnosed with scoliosis and released from active duty. When he arrived home, all he could talk about for months was how he had let down his team, his drill instructors, and himself. His constant talk about how he had abandoned his team continued to frustrate me to the point of almost ruining our relationship. I felt helpless and simply did not understand how or why he was expressing feelings of regret and disappointment over something he had no control."

It was if she had a deep resentment toward the military for the infirmity her son developed, like it was the Marine Corps fault. Oddly, I found myself sympathizing with her. In fact, she feared to lose her son to the military, illness, and perhaps death.

People are unfamiliar with the cultural conditioning in the military and the effect it has on our volunteer force. Some confuse this lost feeling of connectivity (like the woman's son experienced) with post-traumatic stress disorder. I am no psychiatrist, but I do see separation anxiety a little differently than PTSD.

I cannot speak for her son and his experience, but I can talk about my separation from a way of life I loved. Her son spent eight weeks in the military and felt a bond with his comrades. I spent twenty-one years, so I relate to him feeling as though he had let his team and himself down. Despite the distinct difference in the lengths of our enlistments, her son and I can probably appreciate

one another in ways most civilians struggle to understand.

Found in that thread is one of the things I miss about
life in the military: a feeling of belonging to a nobler
objective. Unlike what I see in my civilian counterparts,
the military was more than just a job for me; it was a way
of life.

As this woman concluded the story of her son's military experience, it became evident to me she was merely
sharing her frustration about her very personal encounter with the military. Her unfortunate experience
shaped her opinion about *all* military members.

This story does not have a warm and fuzzy conclu-
sion as I no longer communicate any of my experiences
with her. We come and go like strangers, neither worse
for the wear.

There is a lesson in all of this. Once you identify a
person who is not open to hearing or learning about new
things, particularly your military experiences, consider
different ways of getting your point across without ref-
erencing your time in the Service.

I know, ex-military can sometimes present as arro-
gant know-it-alls, so we must shape our words in ways
that bring down the conversation to a shared level of
comprehension. Attach your message to something the
person already knows and understands, perhaps using
an analogy or personal story with commonalities, then
present it in a non-threatening, amicable way, so the lis-
tener will feel empowered to respond.

Many employers (some work associates too) believe
employees with military backgrounds have a natural

propensity toward responsibility and commitment. That is not to say civilian employees do not have those same traits and corporate environments are devoid of committed professionals. It is only to point out military personnel have been connected to and usually have a strong desire to belong to the greater good.

The importance of the Air Force's constitutional responsibility to the Nation requires its members adhere to higher standards than those expected in civilian life. As Airmen, we are proud of our high standards. Through self-discipline, we adhere to them, and we hold our fellow Airmen accountable to follow our standards.[xxx]

Even though no longer enlisted, I remain bound by those ideals and sometimes hold my peers to the same accountability. These rules of conduct often spill over into the corporate world and right they should; however, we must remember we are no longer in the military when employed as a civilian.

That is easier said than done, I know. Entrenched in our psyche is the belief that the whole is greater than the individual sum of its parts, so we treat our civilian counterparts with an unequivocal level of respect *and* have higher expectations of them. Even contractors who work day to day within military installations have deeply rooted mission-first focus and a heightened sense of purpose.

Not all feel a shared responsibility for the good of the company or the success of an operation. You will encounter those who could give a damn. For some, there is a fine line between acquiescence and defiance. There are unchallenged rules in organizations which infiltrate the ranks. Just like the military, companies adopt un-written standards of conduct, departmental guidelines, and regulations. When a job is on the line, it is difficult to go against the grain; yet, at times you must, even when facing opposition.

However, when you are one of the team you must live up to the rules of conduct instilled in you by your service to our nation. There are times when you must remind yourself how your actions or inactions can make or break the mission. I trust you will always know the difference.

☆ ☆ ☆ ☆ ☆

The Takeaway

I too struggle with being part of an organization that ex-presses things on paper but inconsistently practices the principles they champion. At times, it is equally hard to operate productively within self-restraints let alone corporate constraints. In those instances, you and I must rely on an inner code of conduct: a set of ideologies su-perseding all else. We must remain self-governed with an unbending resolve to serve, honor, and protect the interests of the company as well as our own.

CHAPTER FIVE

LEAD FROM BEHIND

"A leader
is like a shepherd.
He stays behind the flock,
letting the most nimble go out ahead,
whereupon the others follow, not realizing
that all along they are being directed from behind."
Nelson Mandela

No matter how tough you think you are, war will bring out the best and worst of a person. It is hard to witness the aftermath of conflict without walking away affected in some way. There are too many accounts of men and women who are placed in make or break, do, or die situations because of their military experiences.

We have all seen films portraying military officers as the bravest and strongest; however, my personal experience has taught me those depictions are a bit of a stretch. Still, the glory days of actual frontline military officers' leadership moments far outnumber the big-screen outtakes of the past. Purportedly, at the real-life Top Gun program (of which the film is based) there is a five-dollar penalty imposed for any staffer who references or quotes the movie! I wonder what that amount will swell to with a Top Gun sequel in the works!

I long for the days when the top echelon of military leaders was bad-ass and brave! People, despite their titles, have certain characteristics that will either promote or hinder them in their quest to be effective leaders and endear them to their subordinates.

The best leadership advice I ever received came from a man who shared with me two simple words: "Follow me!" He was the epitome of discipline and strength in character. In his simple mandate to follow, he effectively put into action what all good leaders know, which is you lead from behind while appearing to lead from the front. Ancient Chinese philosopher Lao Tzu wrote, "A leader is best when people barely know he exists, when his work is done, his aim fulfilled, they will say: we did it ourselves." Lao Tzu's sage wisdom has, throughout centuries, inspired leaders from around the world. Similarly, shadowing a man I respected and admired, I had a change in underlying assumptions about how to lead, and the trajectory of my life headed in another direction.

But what happens when you encounter or work under people who are inexperienced and do not possess the tactical acumen needed for successful command? Every so often, you will encounter individuals in leadership positions who should not be there.

I clearly remember a newly minted Colonel (O-6) in charge of American heroes: men, and women who had answered our nation's highest call of duty. The Colonel had never worked at a Forward Operating Base (FOB),[xxxi] and once there, her unfamiliarity with tactical operations was abundantly clear. Like General Schwarzkopf once stated, "It doesn't take a hero to order men into battle, it takes a hero to be one who goes into battle." She had neither gone to war nor had charge of anyone outside the classroom.

The Colonel had spent much of her career as a student or an officer in charge of research and development. She might have been the head of her class, but her inexperience in command situations among more experienced subordinates was soon problematic. It was not her fault; she was afforded the position because of her acclaim as a scholar. Her stellar academic record caught the attention of superiors who mistakenly thought she was ready for military command.

Choosing her for a job for which she was unprepared was one of many lessons in leadership failure I experienced while enlisted. Computer scientist and Navy Rear Admiral Grace Murray Hopper wrote "We went overboard on management and forgot about leadership. It might help if we ran the MBAs out of Washington."

Imagine, what a FUBAR it was to put an inexperienced person in charge of genuine American heroes. I am sure you have heard of situations such as hers when a major fail in leadership happens despite an organization's best intentions. For sure, the military has its shortcomings; thus, personnel come and go as in civilian institutions. The rate of attrition is similar in both sectors.

The Colonel's unfortunate predicament reminds me of a story I heard during my active duty days. It is a tale I will always remember.

As the story goes, a promising leader was pegged to take over the role of a retiring Superior. He arrived at his new assignment eager to begin command, with no more than one week to train with his predecessor before the transfer of power. He learned as much as he could in the seven days, at which time he formally took charge of his new company.

Before his predecessor departed, the new hire shared his concerns about being placed in a position of such responsibility. During their final conversation, the new leader asked for any advice the former leader could give him should he find himself in a quandary. The previous leader had pondered for a long time before he gave his replacement an answer.

First, he removed two envelopes from the inside pocket of his jacket. One was labeled #1 and the other #2. He quickly scribbled on two small sheets of paper before placing them separately into the numbered envelopes.

He explained, "When you encounter a situation where you question yourself as a leader these are the exact steps I'd like you to take." He continued, "As soon as you find yourself in a tight spot unsure of what to do, open envelope #1. Then, when you find yourself in another predicament, open envelope #2."

With a smirk, he handed his successor both envelopes before leaving behind all he had cherished for many years. The new hire thanked the outgoing supervisor for his useful advice, bid him farewell, and proceeded to settle in.

After a short time, he became extremely curious as to how the contents of the envelopes would help him get out of a bind when the time came. A few months passed, and his leadership had not yet come into question. He had earned the respect of his subordinates and admiration from his peers. Things were going so well he presumed he might never need the esteemed advice handed down to him by his predecessor.

Nonetheless, while executing a critical tactical operation one day, he found himself questioning his next move, unsure of what to do. Remembering the advice given him, he reached for the envelope labeled #1. He anxiously opened the envelope, confident contained within was the answer to his dilemma. He sat back in his chair, sighed a breath of relief, and read aloud, "When you find yourself in a leadership dilemma with no plausible way out, put the blame on me for anything going awry."

This message was an enormous relief to the new leader. He happily obeyed his predecessor's directive and life for him went on without worry. In his mind, he thanked the retiree for his tremendous show of support, thinking, "How could my predecessor have known his simple instruction would mean so much to me?"

Well, as all time-tested leaders have experienced, it is not *if* you will find yourself in another situation where you question your decisions, it is only a matter of *when*. Sure enough, the new leader found himself in another predicament, and he needed wisdom from the well. He opened the second envelope; confident its contents held the key to his success once more.

His expression turned from gleeful anticipation to despair as he read, "If you are reading this, you are to at once begin typing two more letters for your replacement."

The moral of the story is summed up masterfully with these words from General Bruce D. Clark: "When things go wrong in your command, start searching for the reason in increasingly larger concentric circles around your own desk."

Failures in leadership happen at all levels of authority. Again, memory takes me back to 9/11, the day of the deadliest terrorist attack on U.S. soil. Reportedly, the CIA failed to collaborate with the FBI in its pursuit of two of the al-Qaida-affiliated hijackers. That gloomy day was the beginning of what has now been years of U.S. involvement in the Middle East and the war on terror. Thus, this intelligence misjudgment resulted in the loss of thousands of lives, both here and abroad.

Another failure in the annals of U.S. leadership was the now infamous "Weapons of Mass Destruction (WMD)." A National Intelligence Estimate (NIE) report[xxxii] argued that even though Iraq had a chemical weapons program and the *capability* of producing WMD, there was no substantiating evidence there ever was a stockpile of chemical weapons.

With each of these major accounts, leaders at the highest level, charged with the monumental task of keeping America safe, suffered miscarriages of duty. Despite the epic fail of those whose hands lie our freedoms, as author Bill Fawcett writes, "The world has progressed, technology has grown, and the human race has reached the moon, despite all the errors and stupidities of the past."[xxxiii] The world will forever evolve, regardless of those in charge. Even with preparedness, catastrophes can occur under anyone's watch.

For every blunder in leadership we hear or read about, there are five times as many memorable stories of heroism and courage. History is rife with the accounts of brave men and women who lead our nation in times of war or peace. It is why I am so very proud to be an Airmen as well as an American.

I have personally witnessed many situations where an enlisted hero stands tall in the face of adversity. Many times, these brave men and women do not get deserved recognition. Often, the officer in charge (OIC) gets a good deal of the credit merely for being in charge. An effective leader shares his or her accomplishments with the team. Management expert and prolific author Ken Blanchard wrote, "None of us is as smart as all of us."

I believe not everyone is born to lead, but they may find themselves in charge one day. My biased opinion on this subject elicits the age-old question, "Are good leaders taught how to lead or are they born with the required skills?" One can debate this issue to no end. Let us explore a few perspectives from leaders throughout the ages:

In response to a 1971 Presidio study in military character and leadership,[xxxiv] General Omar Bradley responded, "I would say some [leaders] are born. A person can be born with certain qualities of leadership: good physique, good mental capacity, curiosity, the desire to know....But, there are qualities one can improve on. A thorough knowledge of your profession is the first requirement of leadership and this certainly has to be acquired."

Warren Bennis writes "The most dangerous leadership myth is that leaders are born—that there is a genetic factor to leadership. That's nonsense; in fact, the opposite is true. Leaders are made rather than born."

NFL Championship coach Vince Lombardi said, "Leaders aren't born, they are made. And they are made just like anything else, through hard work. And that's the price we'll have to pay to achieve that goal, or any goal."

Shakespeare wrote, "Some are born great, some achieve greatness, and some have greatness thrust upon them."

Actor Nigel Green says "Leaders aren't necessarily charismatic. They aren't necessarily quiet. There's not a personality trait that will give you a better chance at leading. They're not intuitively extroverted; they're not intuitively introverted. On all the types of characteristics and traits spectrums, there's not one that sticks out. Leadership can be learned."

LeadershipCentral.com, a website where leaders expand and share their knowledge, discusses this very topic in an article aptly titled, *Are Leaders Born or Made.* It asks these provocative questions: "If leaders were born would we have the ability to be a leader in every situation? If we restrict the definition of a leader to only those who express leadership behaviors in all situations within their lives, would we have many leaders?" [xxxv]

Center for Creative Leadership's World Leadership Survey (WLS) also weighed in with a research project interviewing top C-level executives from 53 countries.[xxxvi] The study overwhelmingly concluded people become leaders based on experiences that teach them how to be a leader. I have referenced this study in the resource section at the end of the book. If you, like me, wish to become more effective in your relationships with leaders and your personal progression into the ranks of leadership, I encourage you to read the study. The downloadable PDF offers an enlightening perspective on "borns" versus "mades."

IMD Professor Preston C. Bottger and Research Fellow Jean-Louis Barsoux consider the question "are leaders born or made?" a bad question that incites bad answers.[xxxvii] The scholars further state the question does not consider the level of leadership to which one aspires. There is a hierarchal bent to leadership. A leader at mid-level is perhaps different than one at C-level who is probably different than one who rules a nation.

There are and will always be exceptions to the rule. Love or hate him; President Barack Obama went from a community organizer to a civil rights lawyer to a first term United States Senator to the President of the United States of America. What was it in his character that equipped him to take on one of the highest leadership positions in the world?

Defeated by more than a 2-1 margin in his bid for a congressional seat in the U.S. House of Representatives, he persisted. He went on to deliver one of the nation's most-watched Democratic National Convention keynotes in history before accepting the nomination of his party to run for President of the United States. Some might say, sans experience, he was "born" a leader. Perhaps it was just "the audacity of hope." [xxxviii]

I suggest a worthwhile exercise I once read that may shed light on your capacity to do a job at a higher level of responsibility. First, look at your boss's job and ask if you could do it better.

Next, consider the CEO of the organization and the duties for which he or she is responsible. Get a feel for how you spend your time and energy and honestly evaluate if you are capable of an exponentially heightened degree of responsibility.

Then, make a valid assessment of the role you are pursuing in contrast to your capabilities. Answer as many questions as possible to measure your leadership quotient as well as your wherewithal to manage extreme situations because, above all, a leader must gain, exercise, share, and retain power. Ask yourself these and other questions:

- What are my strengths and weaknesses?
- Have I ever influenced or motivated another to drive positive results?
- Have I shaped a career through mentoring or by representation?
- How do I react to feedback or criticism?
- Has my decision-making ever been tested outside my area of expertise?
- How do others view me?

Undoubtedly, there are many more questions for you to ask and consider. Be thick-skinned and brutally honest in your self-appraisal because not only your future is at stake, but so are others as well as the organization.

Certainly, you will agree that this war-torn topic, discussed *ad nauseam*, still incites conversation. There are thousands of books, articles, blogs, podcasts, and more dedicated to the subject of whether leaders are born or made, with an equal number who choose either side. Perhaps the best response was summarized in the

opening of the article previously cited at Leadership-
Central.com which states, "since we are all born, the best
answer to this question is: leaders are born and then
made!"

As you have seen with the numerous quotes chosen
for this book, the characteristics best framing the leadership traits of men and women are as varied as the authors who wrote them. When reviewing your strengths
and weaknesses to operate at a higher level, do so knowing many leaders conduct a similar self-assessment, and
(re)adjust themselves accordingly.

I share these examples if only to point out the differences of opinions surrounding one single definition or a
precise set of circumstances as it pertains to leadership.
The men and women of The Armed Forces are leaders
every time they leave hearth and home to protect the
freedoms of our nation. However, based on my experiences, there are inconsistencies in the qualities influencing those men and women who I perceive as self-directed and which set us apart:

Resourcefulness

My practices during active duty and the transition process were always proactive. I aggressively engaged (and
continue to do so) in learning opportunities which afforded me an inside peek into the mindset of my superiors. I studied my supervisors carefully and developed
a keen awareness of their positive leadership traits that
helped me interact with them on an [almost] level playing field.

The negative attributes I studied as well, allowing me to play on both sides of the fence. I developed an effective method to deal with my supervisors as well as my peers. Steven Covey wrote, "Management is efficiency in climbing the ladder of success; leadership determines whether the ladder is leaning against the right wall." I knew which was the right wall and proceeded to lean my ladder against it. In the process, I climbed it.

Whether learning comes with traditional education, behind the muzzle of a gun, or on the rungs of a ladder, you must rely on a certain amount of ingenuity, if you want to lead, succeed, and survive.

Confidence

From day one in the Air Force, I knew I was a leader. I needed grade nor position to tell me otherwise. Call it ego, maybe even blind faith; I have always been self-possessed. Growing up in a single-parent household as the oldest of four boys, I understood my role was to speak up for those left voiceless and unheard, even when it was unpopular. I found out as a young child to never be afraid to express myself, but also to know when to turn it down a notch.

As an Airman, I faced life and death decisions that, if I were even the slightest unsure of myself, would have led to irrevocable consequences. Fortunately, my upbringing made me secure in my decisions. I was like General Patton who demanded, "Lead me, follow me, or get out of my way." I knew how to take charge, when to lay back, and with whom to pick my battles. A certain amount of discernment is needed to know when to engage as well as when to walk away from a losing battle.

Ambition

When you stay in the armed forces for 20 or more years, you are immediately eligible to receive a pension based on a percentage of your base pay, despite your age. Usually, it is enough to maintain a modest lifestyle post-military. Keeping that one goal in mind allowed me to successfully navigate more than a two-decade career in the United States Air Force.

All the same, I had other goals like career advancement, education, remaining healthy and in good shape, and staying alive. It may seem trite but when you are in a war zone, returning to your loved ones remains *the* top priority (and a worthy goal). I started a second career post-military, which, as you have now discovered, led to my writing this book.

Integrity

Dwight Eisenhower said, "The supreme quality of leadership is integrity." In the military, I observed a whole lot of, "Do as I say, not as I do" type of behavior that led at times to unfortunate consequences. Some of my superiors, as I am sure many of you have experienced, displayed questionable conduct.

This unfit behavior was commonplace among some supervisors while rank-and-file felt hampered in their response. In fact, between 2004 and 2012, 25% of active

duty Veterans were separated from service due to behavior, performance, legal, and standards of con-
duct.xxxix This number includes all ranks.

There is indeed a fine line between standing up for
yourself and being viewed as insubordinate. Whoever
said men of integrity do not push the envelope is mis-
taken. Men and women of integrity have a duty, a
calling, in fact, to stand up and fight for what is right,
even when it means going against the grain.

When leaders fight for their teams, they earn the respect of peers, subordinates, and other leadership. Leaders, based on their work ethic, courage, empathy, and
valor, are the ones most respected by the people with
whom they work. Like Eisenhower, I too believe the
most important leadership trait is integrity, which is the
combined application of every important characteristic.

Barbara DeAngelis, Ph.D. says living with integrity
means:

- Not settling for less than what you know you deserve in your relationships.
- Asking for what you want and need from others.
- Speaking your truth, even when it might create
  conflict or tension.
- Behaving in ways in harmony with your personal
  values.
- Making choices based on what you believe, and
  not what others believe.

What if [only] distinguished leaders with noble intentions led our soldiers? What if, by the very virtue of serving their country, we exposed all members of the armed

forces to mandatory leadership initiatives that better prepared them for the civilian workforce? I believe there would be lower veteran unemployment after separations, less depression, fewer suicides, and an increase in the retention rate among the military ranks.

I am not implying there are no successful transitions. My story is one of many where preparation met opportunity. The key operative, once again, is preparation. While transitioning, you must confront roadblocks head-on and alter your plan of action as the situations dictate.

Many separated servicemen and women erect powerful platforms from which they excel as professionals in their civilian roles. We prepare for everything and remain receptive to new opportunities. Having a military background allowed me to work better with people in a team environment. Collaboration is critical in extreme environments. You can quit a job, but you cannot just up and leave the military. You can, however, get kicked out, which is why it is crucial to learn about comradery, and how to relate to and understand other people, especially when coming from different social classes.

I know individuals in the military of different races and cultures who I have not seen in ten years, but when seeing them, it is as if we never lost touch. The military friendships and the bonds formed are far beyond the civilian connections I have experienced so far. It cannot be quantified.

I value every aspect of my time in the Air Force. Thus far, my experiences and relationships have proven very helpful to me in the civilian sector. Anything you do to help yourself and those who come after you contribute to your military connected legacy.

☆☆☆☆☆

The Takeaway

If you question whether leadership exists, it is probably absent. You will perhaps find those who are in positions of authority who, for one reason or many, should not be there. Give them the benefit of the doubt but stay away from anyone you do not trust. Abraham Lincoln wrote, "Nearly all men can stand adversity, but if you want to test a man's character, give him power." If veracity is missing, be wary the leader.

I have found when one transitions from the military, it is wise to establish relationships with persons within the company you are considering. Seek out and follow those who are competent, fair, and possess integrity. Learn from them, partner with them, shadow them. Join or form a veteran friendly group that can assist you and others with their transitions. Remain self-directed while standing on the shoulders of those in your inner circle. You will eventually find yourself defining your own leadership style.

CHAPTER SIX

KNOW YOUR WORTH

"Your days
are numbered. Use them
to throw open the windows
of your soul to the sun. If you do not,
the sun will soon set, and you with it."
Marcus Aurelius

Many members of the armed forces separate ill-prepared to face the rigors of a new way of life. Many succumb to low-paying jobs—or worse, unemployment—unable to translate the valuable skills gained as servicemen to a successful, higher-paying civilian career.

The US Department of Veteran Affairs, 2015 Veteran Economic Opportunity Report, revealed about half of all Service members transitioning into civilian life have faced a period of unemployment within 15 months of separation. Although most veterans are entitled to 26 weeks of unemployment benefits, many remain unemployed past their allotment, and this number continues to rise.

Also, veterans under 35 may have difficulty reaching education and employment goals, with vulnerable groups lagging non-Veterans in economic outcomes such as housing and education.[xl]

Those statistics should come as no surprise. For the most part, the TAP is lacking in their support of separating service members. You must proactively seek out reliable people, places, and information to help you with your transition.

There are now more than ever free and low-cost resources to assist you, from books, to websites, to agencies, to individuals. I challenge you to find at least five reliable sources than you feel comfortable referring to as often as needed.

Start networking and find a trusted mentor who understands what you are trying to accomplish. Share with them your frustrations as well as your successes. Use your mentor's wisdom to guide you as you discover your worth—personally, professionally, and financially. As military members, we typically do not know what our value is until we get hired and find out what another associate is earning.

By contrast, employers know very well the value you bring to their organization. George J. Pedersen, Founder, Chairman and CEO of ManTech International Corporation, a leading hirer of transitioning service members writes, "Fifty percent of our employees have a military background. The soldier of today is among the most sophisticated warriors the nation has ever had. The technology they operate and utilize in their missions requires a level of knowledge and training beyond earlier times. Service members also have qualities we need in the workplace—qualities like responsibility, dedication, perseverance, integrity, teamwork, and of course, leadership. We can teach skills on the job or in a classroom, but character is harder to come by."[xli]

In the military, our salaries are based on grade, time, and are public knowledge. Pay is non-negotiable; anyone can find out what you make. So, I never, in my wildest dreams, considered my civilian contemporaries could possibly make more than me for doing the same job and less work. Wrong!

I encourage you to conduct extensive research to ascertain the salary range for the position you are seeking. You would be surprised to learn there might be thousands of dollars between Range A and Range B. Do not leave this to chance. Study every industry, the companies within them, and the employees who work for each.

When evaluating the best field and company fit, reach out to people in the industry you are considering. Strike up salary-based conversations to get a feel for what you can honestly and reasonably expect in compensation. Articulate how your military experiences translate to something the average civilian can both grasp and easily understand. It is your responsibility to explain how your skills can best benefit a company; not the other way around.

You can easily find professionals who are willing to connect with you on LinkedIn. Join industry-specific groups and compile a list of who's who. Find out who the influencers are. Start building relationships with them by commenting on their articles and asking questions related to their fields of expertise.

Another tip is to pay attention to the people in the influencer's network, those who consistently post comments, and those who the influencer references in his or her posts. With a little mining, you might find gold.

Go to meetup.com and find gatherings in your area. If you live in or near a metropolitan area, you will find hundreds of social and business-related meetups. Chances are you will come across others who have similar challenges as you. If you cannot find a group, start one. Identify a need, create the opportunity.

Two overlooked, and underutilized networking venues are your local Chamber of Commerce and SBA/SCORE. Those two entities alone have members who possess a breadth of knowledge from which you can learn, emulate, and trust. The collective wisdom of each group is overwhelming. As a useful side note, part of the TAP is the mandatory Transition, Goals, Success Program (Transition GPS), offering an optional entrepreneurship module that may give you an inside "track" to the SBA programs and grants.

If money is not an issue, consider volunteering with a respected non-profit. You will gain invaluable skills, techniques and methodologies that may prove useful in a future corporate setting.

Consider interning with a stable corporation or technology startup. Both offer significant opportunities for learning, applying new competencies, innovations in technology, prospects for advancement, and growth within the organization. There are numerous ways of adjusting to your changing environment; you must only be willing to go about things differently.

Finally, and only if you are fully committed, go back to school. If you are devoted to offering the highest level of knowledge and hands-on-experience, obtain professional certifications and degrees. Take advantage of your GI Bill and have it work for your future financial security. We live in an increasingly competitive world, not only on a local and national scale but globally. It is wise to develop proficiencies that surpass your contemporaries.

You might consider learning a second or third language. Our nation is quickly becoming bilingual and foreign language classes abound. The need for interpreters and translators remains high on a list of continuously growing occupations. English as a second language (ESL) is an expanding need for many immigrants adapting to America as their new home. Also, with the war on terror, Arabic translators are always in demand. According to the Bureau of Labor Statistics, the job outlook for translators through 2024 has a faster than average growth rate.[xlii]

Meanwhile, healthcare and Information Technology remain high on the list for current and future careers. Most the jobs on U.S. News' "25 Best Jobs of 2017"[xliii] are healthcare-related. Combine translation services, technology, and healthcare, and you may find yourself in a unique career where you can command top dollar.

Medical professions continue to morph into specialization. As well, the world has become less secure than ever before. Cyber warfare is on the rise, and Internet security remains a threat. Likewise, coding, robotics, data, and research analytics have become highly sought-after skills. A profitable future directly correlates with industry demand. Position yourself for careers having the greatest marketability potential.

I wish I could tell you that your military experience is enough to stand on its merit (though it should be), that loyal service to your country will yield a wealth of employment opportunities with promises of a top salary and a fulfilling position. Depending on your area of expertise you should even have an advantage, right?

Unfortunately, as Traditionalists and Baby Boomers age out of the workforce, Millennials remain on the rise. You may find yourself smack dab in the middle, a Generation Xer, like me (according to the Harvard Center this 20-year generation spans from 1965-1984). If so, it is imperative to blend your experience with the old and the new in a way that is both creative and innovative.

Millennials, the largest generation in the American workforce, have advanced technology skills, education, and sufficient practical experience. Do not be surprised if you are subordinate to someone much younger.

Still, glean what you can from those who, young or old, have been where you are trying to get. Act skillfully, exhibit integrity, and you will prime yourself as the ideal candidate for job openings, promotions, and leadership positions.

As you job hunt, skills translators may prove useful when figuring out occupation equivalence in the civilian job marketplace. There are tools available online which will convert military occupational codes (MOC) to related civilian standard professions. Some go even further by taking your skill set, or job functions, and translating them into keywords helpful for you to use on a résumé.

Be aware of your inherent values as you consider the experience, management, and leadership your time in the military has yielded. Do not shy away from what you feel you are worth. Consider everything, i.e., your time, your intellect, your experience, your age, *everything!* If you do not value yourself highly, should you expect a hiring professional to think you are worth more?

Human Resource specialists and recruitment managers are well-trained to present to you the lower end of a pay range. It is in an organization's best interest to find the best person for a job as inexpensively as possible. Still, basic pay and allowances are only a part of the military compensation picture.

Many service members, depending on position and branch, qualify for special and incentives (S&I) that are part of the military's recruitment and retention efforts. Some members receive compensation for hardships or difficult conditions or High Priority Occupations (HPO); hostile fire, hazardous duty, and more. There are over 60 S&I prescribed by law.

The following allowances are necessary to consider when figuring out a comparable civilian salary:

- Housing (not government-provided)
- Subsistence
- Family separation
- Supplemental
- Clothing
- Drill pay

Allowances comprise a significant percentage of a service member's pay, are not taxable, increase an overall compensation package by thousands of dollars, and as such, should be factored into negotiations. Remember also to include the value of benefits, such as bonuses, commissions, health insurance, flexible spending accounts, paid vacation, and Thrift Savings Plans (TSP).

Salary and salary negotiation is left for you to figure out on your own. I did not have a clue what my skills were worth let alone how to negotiate my salary. I offer you this uncomplicated, real-world tutorial because I did not have one. Every principle in this book is battle-tested. It might sound cliché, but again, if it worked for me, it will work for you. There is also a broad range of articles, YouTube videos, podcasts, and more about salary negotiations. We will touch on a few momentarily.

Interview Attire

The clothes we wear often reflects our personality, tradition, and sometimes, budget. And yet, we have all been in professional situations where someone shows up with cringe-worthy attire. But hey, to each his own, right? Wrong. First impressions are powerful. They are also lasting. A misstep in the wardrobe department may close the door to future opportunities with a company. It does not matter if you are responding to a position at a laid-back tech startup or one of the military-friendly corporations in the resource section of this book, do your research and dress appropriately. If you are unsure, ask the person who invites you to the table.

That brings us to the question, should you wear your "dress blues?" There are differing opinions on this subject but consensus advises against it. I too suggest you do not wear your military uniform to a civilian job interview. There are numerous style guides online that speak to this topic. Read the different viewpoints and arrive at your own conclusions.

Keep in mind, I treated myself to new suits and clothes as I accomplished transition goals. There is something about dressing your best that adds to your self-esteem and empowers you to show up. You stand taller, prouder, and more confident.

As well, if you adapt to the established aesthetics of the company for whom you hope to be hired, you might meet with greater success. Do not forget, the dress code for a "prospective" employee is often more conservative than an actual employee. In her insightful article, "What to wear to a job interview"[xliv] Forbes contributor Liz Ryan suggests you "take it up a notch" when interviewing. Research the established dress code for the organization and scale up. You will neither under or over dress in this scenario.

Donna Mayo, owner of seven Liberty Tax franchises, shares another perspective. She is dumbfounded at the number of applicants she turns away each year because of inappropriate attire. She says, "Some women show up wearing leggings and stilettos. I've even had men come for interviews wearing T-shirts and jeans with the smell of cigarettes on their breath." She continues, "I don't care if you are applying to be a tax preparer or the Lady Liberty sign waver, I expect you to come for your interview dressed like the CEO of a major corporation!" She says, "Dressing well speaks volumes about the character of the applicant. We expect our employees to exhibit professionalism in every way at all times."

When all is said, it pays to do your homework. Arrive at your interview on time, smiling, well-dressed, groomed, and prepared. In a weighty pool of candidates, you might be the one who stands out and gets offered the job.

Sign-on Bonus

A civilian sign-on bonus is like a re-enlistment bonus. Not every position merits one nor is it always offered. The same holds true with private organizations. Years ago, you might recall, there was a nursing shortage, and their specialized skills were in high demand. Companies around the country were offering large bonuses for not only experienced nurses but also recent graduates. Most R.N.s could negotiate higher bonuses based on their overall experience and specialties.

Not all companies offer sign on bonuses but you can ask for and receive one simply because you were smart enough to negotiate for it. Surprisingly, one of the things I discovered was with a sign on bonus I could have made over $3000 more my first year. That is money left on the table.

Equally important is knowing when to negotiate a one-time sign on bonus over an increase in yearly salary. You might need the initial outlay of cash, but if you can wait, and if you see yourself at the company long-term, the increased salary probably makes more sense over a one-time bonus. For me, earning three or four thousand dollars per year more over several years instead of a one-time payment is an easy decision! Every situation is different; carefully assess your needs.

Relocation Bonus

Once you have done your homework, do not hesitate to ask about a relocation bonus. I do, however, suggest you use your selective ignorance when inquiring about how much the company is willing to give you and your family to relocate. In other words, ask for the sake of asking. You never know what is available to you if you never open your mouth. Here is one area where civilian companies operate like the military: if you do not ask, they will not tell.

Do not expect a prospective employer to turn over all their cards too early in the interview process. Rarely do they start off or finish with their absolute best offer. Before the job offer, ask for the company's bonus structure. Not only does it show the prospective employer you are proactive, but it also indicates a bonus may be a factor in your decision to take the job. In the same way, it sends a signal you are willing to perhaps hold out for the company offering those bonuses. In this scenario, the employer might not want to lose you.

Which brings us to one of the most important aspects of the civilian job search: when is the best time to begin your salary negotiation?

Salary Negotiations

Save your negotiations until you get an official offer or after you ask for time to consider their proposal. During the interview process *never* answer the questions "What is your current salary?" and "How much are you hoping to make?" Answering either is an automatic "Gotcha!" If you answer with too high a number, you might back yourself out of a potential job. If you answer too low, you will have little to no wiggle room for successful negotiations afterward. Always respond asking a few questions of your own:

- Can you tell me the specifics of the job?
- What is it like working here?

- How many people have you considered for the position?
- Are there other open positions?

Josh Doody, author of Fearless Salary Negotiations,[xlv] suggests asking two or three of these ten job interview questions:

1. What does a typical day look like for this role?
2. What is the greatest challenge for the role?
3. What is the company culture?
4. Where is the company headed?
5. How has the company changed in the past year?
6. Can you tell me about the team?
7. Is the team working on any special projects?
8. Can you tell me about career growth opportunities?
9. What do you like best about working here?
10. What are the expectations of this role during the first 90 days?

I am sure you get the picture. You will only need to counter with a few questions before the interviewer realizes you are not going to answer the dreaded money question. The key here is to gather intel about a position so you can figure out what is required of you to excel in the position. It is easier to determine the value of a job when you know what it will demand.

When you are in the hot seat, it is uncomfortable to turn the table. But, I have also found when you remain in control of the interview, it is less stressful and ultimately goes in your favor. So, relax. Display confidence. Stick to your guns and do not be the first to buckle.

You are strong. You are proud. You have served in the United States Armed Forces. You have withstood the rigors of intense training, terrorism, war, natural disasters, and acts of God. Your country demanded the best of you, and you delivered! That is reason enough to hold your head high and demand your worth. Do your due diligence beforehand, show up prepared, and do not settle!

In the Art of War, Sun Tzu wrote: "So the important thing in a military operation is victory, not persistence."[xlvi] I say, "The most important aspect of your shift from military to civilian is a victorious transition using planned persistence."

There is a Spanish saying, *La esperanza es lo último que se pierde* which means "hope is the last thing you lose."

I hope that you, the civilian reading this account, now have a better understanding of factors influencing an ex-military member's mindset and job performance. I also hope you have had a few "light bulb" moments that will help you become a better, higher-paid manager and leader in your field of expertise.

Finally, to the military member, I have every confidence you will get everything out of this life you desire if you put forth both the effort and the resolve. You have put your lives on the line for a country you and I both love. Now, when you need it most, I hope this country pays you in diamonds. You deserve it!

ACRONYMS

Following is a list of acronyms used throughout the book. Some acronyms are universal while others identify with the branch of service.

2IC	Second in Charge
ACAP	Army Career and Alumni Program
AFB	Air Force Base
AFSC	Air Force Specialty Code
AFGM	Air Force Guidance Memorandum
AFRC	Airman and Family Readiness Centers
AIT	Advanced Individual Training
ALS	Airmen Leadership School
ASVAB	Armed Services Vocational Aptitude Battery Test
CEO	Chief Executive Officer
CRM	Crew Resource Management
DOD	Department of Defense
DTM	Directive-Type Memorandum
DVA	Department of Veterans Affairs
ENT	Ear, Nose, and Throat
ESL	English as a Second Language
EPR	Enlisted Performance Report
ETS	Expiration-Term of Service
FNG	F*cking New Guy
FOB	Forward Operating Base
FRAGOs	Fragmentary Orders

FUBAR	F*cked Up Beyond Any Recognition
GOBI	General Officer Bright Idea
HPO	High Priority Occupation
HUA	Head up a$$
IED	Improvised Electronic Device
KISS	Keep it Simple Stupid
LEAD	Leaders Encouraging Airmen
MBA	Master of Business Administration
MBTI	Myers-Briggs Type Indicator®
MOC	Military Occupational Codes
MOS	Military Occupational Specialty
MRM	Maintenance Resource Management
NCO	Non-Commissioned Officer
NCOA	Non-commissioned Officer Academy
NCOIC	Non-commissioned Officer in Charge
NIE	National Intelligence Estimate
OIC	Officer in Charge
OJT	On the Job Training
ORM	Operational Risk Management
PCP	Primary Care Physician
PCS	Permanent Change of Station
PGA	Professional Golfers Association
PME	Professional Military Education
PPE	Personal Protective Equipment
PTRP	Physical Therapy Rehabilitation Platoon
PTSD	Post-Traumatic Stress Disorder
PV2	Private Second Class
QDC	Quality, Delivery, Cost
ROTC	Reserved Officer Training Corps
S&I	Special and Incentives
SAT	Scholastic Aptitude Test

SNAFU	Situation Normal All F*cked Up
SNCOA	Senior Non-Commissioned Officer Academy
SOP	Standard Operating Procedures
SWOT	Strengths, Weaknesses, Opportunities, and Threats
TAP	Transition Assistance Program
TDY	Temporary Duty
TOWS	Threats to Opportunities, Weaknesses to Strengths
TSP	Thrift Savings Plan
TWI	Training Within Industry
UCMJ	Uniform Code of Military Justice
USC	United States Code
VA	Veterans Affairs
VBOP	Veterans Business Outreach Program
VEI	Veteran's Employment Initiative
VMET	Verification of Military Experience and Training
VOW	Veterans Opportunity to Work (Act)
VSO	Voluntary Service Organization
WLS	World Leadership Survey
WMD	Weapons of Mass Destruction
WTF	What the F*ck
WTU	Warrior Transition Unit

RESOURCES

Government Agencies

U.S. Department of Veterans Affairs
The VA is your first stop in a long line of (official) organizations beneficial to your transition. It is chock full of needed resources for the enlisted and separated service member. There are local facilities in most parts of the country.
https://www.va.gov/

National Institute for Mental Health

It is no secret many military members have PTSD. Symptoms are severe for some veterans, interfering with relationships, work, and quality of life. If you feel you are suffering from any mental health issue, talk to your VA advocate for guidance.
https://www.nimh.nih.gov/index.shtml

Small Business Association

Not every transitioning veteran will want to go the corporate route as an employee. If you would like to transition into entrepreneurship, the SBA has several programs and resources to help you accomplish your dream of self-employment and business ownership. The Veterans Business Outreach Program (VBOP) provides entrepreneurial development services for

eligible veterans owning or considering starting a small business.
https://www.sba.gov/

The Wounded Warrior Project

Whether newly injured or on the path to recovery, WWP will support you as you define your new normal.
https://www.woundedwarriorproject.org/

Organizations

IMD are experts on developing global leaders, offering a free tool allowing you to benchmark your leadership skills, helping you identify traits that need improving and strengthening.
https://global-leader-index.imd.org/

The Arbinger Institute, founded in 1979, has worked with thousands of individuals and organizations to transform performance and help change mindsets. The white paper (PDF), "Dramatically Improving Performance" can be downloaded here:
https://arbinger.com/wp-content/uploads/2013/10/2015-WHITE-PAPER-Dramatically-Improving-Performance.pdf

Books

"Not all readers are leaders, but all leaders are readers."
Harry S. Truman

The 48 Laws of Power
Robert Greene, a Joost Elffers Production, Penguin
This national bestseller is one of the best roadmaps to leadership I know. The author has an uncanny ability to juxtapose those who lead against those who desire to do so. This comprehensive book uses a vast arsenal of quotes, first person accounts, research, and more. It is certain to shift your perspective on leadership and what it takes to acquire and maintain it.

The Powell Principles, 24 Lessons from Colin Powell, Battle-Proven Leader
Oren Harari, McGraw-Hill
I refer to this book a couple of times in *Stewards of Excellence*. General Powell is a respected leader who has repeatedly performed under fire and withstood the test. The strategies used throughout his successful military career serve as a roadmap for any person hoping to achieve an unmatched level of success in his or her career.

On Becoming a Leader: The Leadership Classic
Warren Bennis, Basic Books
We referred to Professor Bennis' body of work a few times throughout the book. Regarded as one the foremost authorities in the contemporary field of leadership, Bennis, one of the youngest infantry

commanders in Germany, was awarded the Purple Heart and Bronze Star. *On Becoming a Leader* examines the qualities of leadership and the strategies to apply to become an effective leader.

Outliers: The Story of Success
Malcolm Gladwell, Little, Brown, and Company
In Outliers, Malcolm Gladwell tackles wealth, privilege, and class to prove the relational traits of each as defined by the community. I am an outlier, separated at birth from those of privilege, yet bound by the same promise as others in my pursuit of happiness and the American Dream. My slant toward leadership and ultimately to the success in which it leads is unique and based on my reality. Outliers is a must read for anyone trying to establish their place in a changing world.

The Audacity of Hope: Thoughts Reclaiming the American Dream
Barack Obama, Three Rivers Press
Regardless of your political or cultural views, this book speaks to a determined spirit in each of us to pursue freedom, democracy, justice, and the American Dream.

The 21 Irrefutable Laws of Leadership: Follow Them and People Will Follow You
John C. Maxwell, Thomas Nelson Publishers
A top-selling leadership book with over a million copies sold, John Maxwell has indisputably positioned himself as a globally recognized leadership expert. His well-researched subject matter is a go-to source for leveraging a successful career, in and outside the

boardroom. As Steven Covey surmises in the book's introduction, "it [the book] will change the way you live and lead."

The 7 Habits of Highly Effective People: Powerful Lessons in Personal Change
Steven R. Covey, Simon & Schuster
In this ground-breaking bestseller, which has sold over 20 million copies worldwide, Mr. Covey teaches us authentic success is a balance of personal and professional effectiveness. He challenges us to look at life in an uncommon way and rethink how the world works. Doing so opens an entirely new world of possibilities. His time-proven lessons are still applicable in today's competitive workplace.

The Self-Made Billionaire Effect: How Extreme Producers Create Massive Value
John Sviokla and Mitch Cohen, Portfolio/Penguin
I happened across this book at a seminar a few years ago, where I met Mitch, now retired Vice-Chairman PwC - PricewaterhouseCoopers. In the book, the author(s) define the profound difference in mindset between "performers" and "producers." With an overwhelming slant toward the "producers," they show how producers trust their instincts enough to make lasting organizational changes.

The Seven Spiritual Laws of Success: A Practical Guide to the Fulfillment of Your Dreams
Deepak Chopra, Amber-Allen Publishing
Dr. Chopra uses timeless wisdom and logical steps to help you take a different perspective on success. He

shows us it is not only what we know but how deeply we believe in our true nature that sets us up for success. A quick, engrossing read.

Winning
Jack Welch with Suzy Welch, Harper Business
Warren Buffett writes, "No other management book will ever be needed." Retired CEO of GE, Welch, known throughout the world as a leading authority in management and leadership practices, has broad-spectrum appeal. His down-to-earth message resonates with individuals at each level of an organization, from non-specialists to C-Suite executives.

Band of Brothers: E Company, 506th Regiment, 101st Airborne from Normandy to Hitler's Eagle's Nest
Stephen E. Ambrose, Simon & Schuster
World War II historian Stephen Ambrose tells the riveting story of Easy Company's group of elite paratroopers from basic training to war casualties to triumph. The author allows a penetrating glimpse into the interrelations of soldiers and their commanding officers, life in combat in foreign lands, and more. This popular book, made into an HBO original miniseries, won critical acclaim and awards.

Awaken the Giant Within: How to take immediate control of your mental, emotional, physical & financial destiny!
Anthony Robbins, Summit Books
Tony Robbins is one of today's leading-edge, world-acclaimed peak performance coaches. His best-selling books, sold-out seminars, and private training sessions

offer innovative technology for the management of human emotion and behavior. This classic volume is chock full of strategies to stir your spirit and awaken the giant within.

The Art of War
Sun Tzu, Chiron Academic Press, Amazon Digital Services
This free, downloadable book shares timeless insights into strategy, goal-setting, and achievement. Not only is it a well-respected military guide, over the years it has become the quintessential management bible, offering inspiration and advice on how to succeed in competitive situations.

See You at the Top: The "How to" book that gives you a "Checkup" from the "Neck Up" to eliminate "Stinkin Thinkin" and AVOID "Hardening of the Attitudes."
Zig Ziglar, Pelican Publishing Company
Zig Ziglar is perhaps the king of personal motivation. Through the imaginative stories he shares, he compels readers to get rid of negativity and replace it with ideals of character and integrity, ingredients for leadership. Ziglar's book illustrates how changing the way you think is the direct path to improving how you do things. He writes, "Because we believe—and love—our purpose in life is to help you help yourself."

Handbook of Organizations
James G. March, Routledge
This comprehensive, weighty, academic tome is for anyone serious about organizational theory and

leadership. It is rich in historical data, concepts, ideas, theories, and evidence-based best practices. With numerous chapters focusing on leadership, I recommend downloading the free version and referring to it often.

As you know, there is an endless list of quality books, more than pages allow us to reference here. Goodreads offers a reader-curated list of the top military-inspired leadership books:
https://www.goodreads.com/shelf/show/military-leadership

Websites

The Defense Finance and Accounting arm of the DoD provides essential knowledge about your pay, benefits, and more. This site is necessary during your transition planning stage and beyond. Even if you have a responsible advocate helping you transition, having firsthand knowledge is always a good idea.
https://www.dfas.mil/retiredmilitary.html

U. S. Department of Defense has an A-Z list of every DoD sanctioned website and social media account. If you are looking for a branch, department, or service, this is where you will find it.
https://www.defense.gov/About/Military-Departments/A-Z-List

U.S. Department of Defense Military Compensation is your source for all things pay, including benefits, incentives, allowances, retirement, and more.
http://militarypay.defense.gov/

GI Jobs Their mission is to simplify the military transition experience using tools and resources to guide you to a successful career. Bookmark this site and refer to it often.
http://www.gijobs.com/about-us/

Military Times shares useful information for military past, present, and future. It is chock full of history, current affairs, education, career advice, and more.
http://www.militarytimes.com/

Military.com has a broad range of subject matter to enhance your transition planning. A good website to bookmark.
http://www.military.com/military-transition/my-transition-plan

Oxford Handbooks Online also offers *The Oxford Handbook of Leadership and Organization's abstracts and keywords*. A very useful research site.
http://www.oxfordhandbooks.com/view/10.1093/oxfordhb/9780199755615.001.0001/oxfordhb-9780199755615

The Free Management Library has grown to be one of the world's largest collections of management articles and resources about personal, professional, and organizational development. Here for you is an

abundance of material to aid you in your pursuit of the ideal career and professional development.
http://managementhelp.org/leadership/index.htm

TED is a nonprofit devoted to spreading ideas in the form of short talks. The organization has grown in stature and influence over the years and now boasts an impressive library of topics from some the world's greatest thought leaders, change agents, scholars, storytellers, and more. Check out these leadership talks.
https://www.ted.com/topics/leadership

Leadership-Central is where leaders expand and share their knowledge. A great resource for getting different points of view on leadership-related topics. Page after page on communications, motivation, leadership theories, time management, and more. You will want to bookmark this site.
http://www.leadership-central.com/#axzz4ZONRuwqN

The 2016 Air Force Chief of Staff Reading List
The site is a virtual library of leadership inspired, success related books, films, TED Talks, and more. It is a curated list created in 1996 by General Ronald Fogleman helping Air Force members become more effective advocates.
http://static.dma.mil/usaf/csafreadinglist/01_books.html

Military Friendly Employers

Forbes Magazine listed the top 50 military-friendly employers.[xlvii] These are a few based on their findings:

Combined Insurance is committed to individuals with a military background, dedicated to hiring over 2,800 veterans and providing them with meaningful career opportunities by the end of 2017.
http://www.combinedinsurance.com/us-en/Careers/Career-for-Veterans.aspx

USAA Banking, insurance, and investment company supporting our nation's military men and women by maintaining a 30% military and military spouse hiring goal. The company provides numerous programs to attract, support, train, educate, and develop military talent.
https://www.usaajobs.com/military/

Baker Hughes is a high-performance drilling, production technology, and services company that appreciate the contributions, discipline, and commitment to hard work military members provide.
https://public.bakerhughes.com/Military/military-jobs

Union Pacific operates North America's premier railroad franchise. The company looks for employment candidates with a military member's leadership and adaptability skills to join their teams.
https://up.jobs/transitioning-veterans.html

Allied Universal is the largest provider of security services in North America. Military hiring is an essential part of AU's recruiting strategy.
http://www.aus.com/Careers

CSX is one of the nation's leading transportation suppliers. The company actively seeks employees with military service experience.
https://www.csx.com/index.cfm/working-at-csx/learn-more-about-csx/military-friendly-employer/

J.B. Hunt Transportation Service understands the value a military background brings to their company. One in five J.B. Hunt employees is a military veteran.
https://www.jbhunt.com/jobs/military/

Schneider National is a part of the Department of Veterans Affairs (VA) Apprenticeship Program. You can use your education benefits for training *and* receive a paycheck from Schneider.
https://schneiderjobs.com/company-drivers/military/apprenticeship-program

Sutter Health is comprised of more than 50,000 doctors, employees, and volunteers. They welcome employees who bring diverse backgrounds and perspectives that reflect the communities they serve. Sutter offers internships, fellowships, and residencies. They also have helpful resources on their website for job applicants and employment candidates.
http://www.sutterhealth.org/employment/

ManTech International Corporation is a member of the Veteran Jobs Mission, a coalition of companies aiming to hire 1 million U.S. military veterans.
http://www.mantech.com/careers/Pages/military.aspx

Verizon was ranked #1 by Military Times. The website has a skills match tool, list of military recruiters, and other essentials to aid you in your transition.
http://www.verizon.com/about/careers/military

Other

Veteran's Crisis Line 1-800-273-8255 Press 1
This Hotline connects Veterans in crisis, their families, and friends with supportive DVA responders. Calls are confidential.

National Suicide Prevention Lifeline

1-800-273-TALK (8255)

The National Suicide Prevention Lifeline is a network of local crisis centers providing free and confidential emotional support to people in suicidal crisis or emotional distress 24 hours a day, seven days a week.

National Domestic Violence Hotline

1-800-799-SAFE (7233)

Every man and woman deserves to be safe. If you are or know of someone abused in any way, please get, or offer help.

I am sure there are substantially more books and resources that have helped you in your personal life, leadership journey, and military transition. I would love to know the tools you have used to aid you in your transition or career, whether books, organizations, speakers, training, or other.

Connect with me on LinkedIn where I share tips and strategies to help your transition be the most successful it can be. Join the conversation.

Lastly, would you please leave a short review on Amazon? If you have benefited from any of the information shared in this book, please let me and others know.

ABOUT THE AUTHOR

Roderick Steward, USAF, (Ret.) B.S., CPM, LSSBB retired from the United States Air Force after 21-years of active duty. He was a Human Factors Engineer Master Instructor for Air Force Aerospace and Operational Physiology/Human Factors, Maintenance Resource Management (MRM), Operational Risk Management (ORM), Security Forces Ground Combat, Crew Resource Management (CRM), and Human Performance Enhancement. He is well versed in risk, strategy, instructional systems design, and project management.

Mr. Steward is a seasoned Lean Six Sigma Black Belt, Senior Lean Executive Coach and Consultant with a Bachelor's degree in Technical Management from Embry-Riddle Aeronautical University. He is also a Certified Public Manager from the University of Texas.

Passionate about helping newly separated veterans and transition teams, Human Resources Departments, and rank-and-file establish a framework for success, Roderick travels extensively speaking before enthusiastic audiences. He trains engaged participants nationwide with a mix of humor, wit, and hands-on applications, helping them further excel in their positions.

Born in Houston, Texas to Elaine Steward, Roderick now resides in California, playing golf, parachuting, riding motorcycles, and spending time with family and friends in his spare time.

THE AIRMAN'S CREED

I am an American Airman.
I am a Warrior.
I have answered my Nation's call.
I am an American Airman.
My mission is to Fly, Fight, and Win.
I am faithful to a Proud Heritage,
A Tradition of Honor,
And a Legacy of Valor.
I am an American Airman.
Guardian of Freedom and Justice,
My Nation's Sword and Shield,
Its Sentry and Avenger.
I defend my Country with my Life.
I am an American Airman.
Wingman, Leader, Warrior.
I will never leave an Airman behind,
I will never falter,
And I will not fail.

REFERENCES

[i] http://www.inc.com/jeff-haden/the-top-50-leadership-and-management-experts-mon.html

[ii] https://en.wikipedia.org/wiki/Loss_aversion

[iii] http://www.academyadmissions.com/admissions/advice-to-applicants/enlisted-airmen/

[iv] America's Air Force: A Profession of Arms "The Little Blue Book (e-publishing.af.mil, 2015)

[v] http://mldc.whs.mil Military Leadership Diversity Commission Issue Paper #6 Definition of Diversity

[vi] https://www.usfa.fema.gov/downloads/pdf/code_of_ethics.pdf

[vii] https://en.wikipedia.org/wiki/Emergency_workers_killed_in_the_September_11_attacks

[viii] http://www.militaryfactory.com/vietnam/casualties.asp

[ix] http://www.ptsd.va.gov/public/PTSD-overview/basics/history-of-ptsd-vets.asp

[x] https://steveblank.com/2014/01/14/whats-a-pivot/

[xi] http://www.militaryonesource.mil/phases-retiring?content_id=267523

[xii] http://www.ibisworld.com/

[xiii] http://www.myersbriggs.org/

[xiv] http://warfarehistorynetwork.com/daily/military-history/what-makes-great-commanders-great/

[xv] Oren Harari, The Powell Principles, 24 Lessons from Colin Powell, Battle-Proven Leader, 2015, McGraw Hill Books

[xvi] Hill, Napoleon, Think and Grow Rich, 1937 edition, Sound Wisdom. Official Publication of the Napoleon Hill Foundation, 2016 edition

[xvii] http://diversity.defense.gov/Portals/51/Documents/Resources/Commission/docs/Issue%20Papers/Paper%2006%20-%20DOD%20Core%20Values.pdf

[xviii] http://www.armystudyguide.com/content/the_tank/army_report_and_message_formats/fragmentary-order-frago.shtml

[xix] http://jamesclear.com/lay-a-brick

[xx] Owings, Tim, Cadence of Care: Imagining a Transformed Advisor-Client Experience, 2016, Stroud & Hall Publishers Pg.30

[xxi] Biological Sciences - Psychological and Cognitive Sciences - Social Sciences - Psychological and Cognitive Sciences: Robb B. Rutledge, Nikolina Skandali, Peter Dayan, and Raymond J. Dolan A computational and neural model of momentary subjective well-being PNAS 2014 111 (33) 12252-12257; published ahead of print August 4, 2014, doi:10.1073/pnas.1407535111

[xxii] http://www.usnews.com/education/blogs/mba-admissions-strictly-business/2011/05/27/moving-from-the-military-to-business-school

[xxiii] http://www.cbsnews.com/feature/va-hospitals-scandal/

[xxiv] http://www.ehow.com/info_7934114_happens-hurt-basic-training.html Recycling

[xxv] https://www.justice.gov/opa/pr/justice-department-recovers-38-billion-false-claims-act-cases-fiscal-year-2013

[xxvi] https://www.acap.army.mil/

[xxvii] http://www.benefits.va.gov/compensation/)

[xxviii]http://www.publichealth.va.gov/exposures/agentorange/conditions/index.asp

[xxix] Les Wallace, James Trinka, A Legacy of 21st Century Leadership: A Guide for Creating a Climate of Leadership Throughout Your Organization, 2007, iUniverse, Inc.

[xxx] By Order of the Air Force Instruction, 1-1. (n.d.). Retrieved from http://static.epublishing.af.mil/production/1/af_cc/publication/afi1-1/afi1-1.p

[xxxi]http://www.globalsecurity.org/military/library/report/2006/ssi_wong-gerras.pdf

[xxxii]http://nsarchive.gwu.edu/NSAEBB/NSAEBB129/nie_first%20release.pdf

[xxxiii] http://www.huffingtonpost.com/bill-fawcett/10-of-the-greatest-leader_b_2057685.html

[xxxiv] Nineteen Stars: A Study in Military Character & Leadership, (CA: Presidio, 1971), by Edgar F. Puryear, Jr.

[xxxv] http://www.leadership-central.com/are-leaders-born-or-made.html#ixzz4SK8abbMc

[xxxvi] https://www.ccl.org/wp-content/uploads/2015/02/AreLeadersBornOrMade.pdf

[xxxvii] http://www.imd.org/research/challenges/TC022-10.cfm

xxxviii Obama, Barack, The Audacity of Hope: Thoughts on Reclaiming the American Dream, 2006, Three Rivers Press, New York

xl http://www.benefits.va.gov/benefits/docs/veteraneconomicoppor tunityreport2015.pdf, 2.6 Reason for Separation

xli http://www.mantech.com/careers/Pages/military.aspx

xlii https://www.bls.gov/ooh/media-and-communication/interpreters-and-translators.htm

xliii http://money.usnews.com/money/careers/slideshows/the-25-best-jobs-of-2017?slide=26

xliv https://www.forbes.com/sites/lizryan/2015/03/21/what-to-wear-to-a-job-interview/2/#39ad2bc46e15

xlv https://fearlesssalarynegotiation.com/10-good-questions-to-ask-in-a-job-interview/

xlvi Tzu, Sun, The Art of War, 2007, Filiquarian

xlvii https://www.forbes.com/pictures/fjle45jhgk/the-top-50-military-friendly-employers/#2b9ac073185c